DIVORCE:

A
SURVIVOR'S
GUIDE

NANCY J. WELLS

Divorce: A Survivor's Guide

© 2023 Nancy J. Wells

ISBN 978-1-66786-664-2

eBook ISBN 978-1-66786-665-9

Dedication

I dedicate this book to my beautiful family and friends who picked me up off the floor and stood watch over me until I could stand on my own.

CONTENTS

Introduction

I've given a lot of thought on how to address my ex-husband in this writing. Contenders are:

- Leech
- Viper
- Bloodsucker
- Piece of Shit

I don't want to sound bitter. I would not have used those adjectives to describe him prior to our divorce but truth is truth. His true nature and his character were revealed throughout the divorce proceedings. All the above adjectives are the absolute truth, and many similar others would apply as well. Unfortunately, those adjectives do not represent even a microscopic portion of the havoc and misery he caused.

I think I'll go with Piece of Shit, or POS. It's short, sweet, and easy to remember. My ordeal has earned me the right to use that name. When I referenced him as such, my family suggested I use that acronym in my story. Piece of Shit. It's spot on.

Maybe I'll have a contest for readers to offer their own suggestions. But before suggesting alternative names, you'll need to know what happened.

Here we go.

Chapter 1:
And So It Begins

When I started to write this book, I had just come back from my attorney's office where I had finally signed my Separation Agreement, which is just one document among the many involved in the journey to a divorce. Divorce is all about documents. There are papers, worksheets, forms, discovery requirements, motions, and court filings, which all lead up to the ultimate document – a Judgement of Divorce, better known as a divorce decree.

Heaven vs. Hell, or Should I Just Say Hell

Divorce is emotional, unsettling, stressful, and messy from beginning to end. In divorce you experience multiple emotions at once, in a minute-by-minute ever-changing kaleidoscope. Emotional highs and lows and everything in between. You're making legal and life-changing decisions while your emotions are spiking and plummeting. To be overwhelmed is a given. Recognize that divorce is trauma. Whether it catches you by surprise or it's something you want, it unsettles your life.

If you were to ask, "Is it possible to have a smooth divorce?" I would say that yes, it is. I have had the experience of divorce twice in my life, both in New York State. My first divorce was 25 years ago, and it was a smooth one. We went to a mediator four times. My first ex-husband and I met with the mediator to understand what needed to be included in the Separation Agreement. We agreed on the details at home and advised the mediator, who drew up the paperwork. Once we signed the papers, the mediator filed them with the court. That's it. It was relatively easy-peasy. The legal paperwork was mostly generic and straightforward, even allowing for custody of our daughter, child support, and separation of house assets.

Afterwards, my first ex-husband and I co-parented our daughter very well. My goal was to raise her in an environment with as little divorce stress as possible. Check your issues at the door. Of course, for this strategy to work both people must be somewhat sane human beings. He remarried and I consider him, his wife, and their children to be family. People are surprised regarding our cordial relationship. Acting like adults was best not only for my daughter, who was 4 years old at the time, but for their kids as they came along. I'm very proud of the great job we all did as a team.

Apologies for going off topic for a bit. My point was to demonstrate that a smooth divorce, and even a smooth post-divorce, is possible. Smooth is nice and I hope your divorce is smooth. It would be a blessing and a kindness if the legal aspects of your divorce were smooth, leaving you more bandwidth to heal and move on.

A smoother divorce minimizes trauma and allows you to get acclimated to your new normal and focus on rebuilding your life. Perhaps you can't get to a completely smooth divorce, but even small steps toward a smoother divorce would help.

But some divorces are not smooth. And not just un-smooth, but pretty damn awful. Of the divorces which fall into the awful category I expect there are many levels of awfulness, ranging from just slightly awful to horror movie awful. My recent second divorce was one of those. It was the polar opposite of smooth and I would rate it as horror movie awful. And as I discovered, the alternative of a smooth divorce can grind you into the ground.

The first thing you feel at the thought of a divorce is panic. Once I knew divorce was inevitable, I was, as expected, greatly upset over the breakup of my marriage. However, my panic was exponentially multiplied, and I was close to hysterical over what I knew was headed my way in the divorce. Knowing my spouse, I knew what I was in for, and how bad he would make it. My apprehension was off the charts. It turned out worse than I imagined. I have since learned what a nightmare it is to divorce someone who fights dirty.

In our marriage I thought I was exempt from the indifference the POS showed to the rest of the world. That was terribly naïve of me. His indifference turned into callousness, which then turned into plain old malice, expressed through gaslighting and bullying. It was a hard lesson to learn and live through. It's reflective of his character, and his traits were displayed in full force throughout the divorce proceedings.

My recent divorce took two years to complete. Twenty-four long months of silence on the home front, money worries, money payments, and money wasted. Twenty-four months of strategy discussions, legal options, and thousands of emails. All mixed in with emotional trauma like I had never experienced. In my case, it was 24 months of protecting myself from layer upon layer of lies, nastiness, and hate thrown at me, both from my spouse and his Barracuda attorney. Their cutthroat tactics did everything and anything to guarantee a hellish divorce.

My case was 17 months of maneuvering through a grueling divorce process to get to a Separation Agreement, followed by 7 months to get the Judgement of Divorce. It was a long, tedious, and painful process. Two years of him playing dirty, living in my house free of charge, and taking financial advantage of me anyway he could. Months which felt even longer with no end in sight, or should I say, no immediate end in sight. Sometimes making the right decision, sometimes making the wrong one, and sheer hell all the way.

Based on his personality and how he handled conflict, I knew the POS was going to go for the jugular. The famous Bette Davis quote "Fasten your seatbelts, it's going to be a bumpy night" from *All About Eve* (Zanuck & Mankiewicz, 1950) perfectly described my situation and dread for the entire time it took to get to a signed Separation Agreement.

From beginning to end, it was a bare-knuckle cage match.

The D Word

You hear about divorce all the time. On TV, social media, everywhere. It is a worldwide phenomenon with hundreds, thousands, and millions going through it every day. Marital trauma on a global scale. However, knowing the volume of people going through it doesn't lessen your feelings. Everyone experiences the divorce fallout of fear, loss, and grief. Even if you want the divorce, you cannot avoid feeling the loss of a marriage. Our hearts and minds are not a light switch which can be turned quickly on or off, even if we wish it was so. It's a painful process all around.

Divorce is global, not just throughout the world, but global in your life. Your whole life is changing, your future path may be unknown, and you can't pretend otherwise. It includes your relationships, children, finances, career, where you live, how you live, and expectations for the future. Every holiday, weekend, and simply everyday life is different. It feels different living inside your own skin and that can be tough to come to terms with.

Being divorced means you're now in a different category. You joined The Divorced Club. People see you differently, and you'll see yourself differently. Your pre-divorce life is gone, to be replaced by a different post-divorce life. You'll mourn your pre-divorce life. I know I did, and still do at times. But I'm learning that life is long, that you can recover and move on.

Currently you're in the pre – or mid-divorce phase. First, let me say I'm sorry for the difficult path you're on. Your goal is to get through the process and to come out the other side somewhat whole. Perhaps not entirely whole, but as whole as you can possibly make it. And after it's over, to settle into your new changed life, adding bits and pieces back in to become even more whole. What you feel after the first week will be different from what you will feel after the first six months, or year, or years to come.

What is the ultimate objective for the divorce? Only one thing...to get out alive!

The Process of Divorce

As laymen to the legal proceedings and complications of a divorce, the average person requires a lawyer to help guide them through the divorce process. Your lawyer will speak a different language than you, a language used in the numerous discussions on strategy and various legal documents. A new language that you will become more familiar with as you progress.

Along the way you will be asked to make decisions regarding strategy. A divorce attorney does not dictate the decisions for your case. They discuss legal options with you and are guided by how you want to proceed. It is very much a team effort between you and your attorney.

Although all divorces have different circumstances with different players, the process of divorce remains the same.

Learning about an unfamiliar process helps to reduce anxiety. That's why healthcare providers explain what is going to happen in medical procedures. It prepares you for what is ahead, and the additional understanding helps to calm fears. If you know what to expect, you can go through it with less anxiety and hopefully a clearer mind. The same theory applies to a divorce. You will be less surprised, better prepared, and hopefully make better choices knowing what is next in the divorce process.

I am not a writer, or an attorney, or a therapist. I'm an average woman who has been through the New York State divorce courts. Twice. I'm not necessarily proud of that fact, but there it is. I write of my recent divorce not so much as a how-to, or as a how-not-to, but as a be-aware-as-you-go. Perhaps knowing someone else's story can benefit your own. My experience can help make sense out of confusion as you navigate your own path along the yellow brick road of divorce.

Key Take-Aways:

Your world is changing.

It's okay to grieve over the loss of your marriage.

You are not alone.

Take a deep breath.

How bad is it going to be?

Oh no.

There are reasonable divorces, and then there is hell.

Take my experience and apply as needed.

No judgement if you need some ice cream.

Chapter 2:
So.... How Do You Get Divorced?

The legal objective of divorce is to separate a married couple's property into two separate buckets. This distribution process includes assets, physical property, and debts. The first thing to understand is what legal guidelines would apply to your divorce. Where your divorce is filed determines which type of distribution guidelines are applicable in your divorce. Legal guidelines are determined by the state processing your divorce.

Community Property State vs Equitable Distribution State

For the division of property, states are either a community property state or an equitable distribution state. How divorce is processed in your state will impact your case since different rules apply for each method.

In a community property state, property is divided equally for anything acquired by either spouse during the marriage. Everything is a 50/50. Community property states are:

- Arizona
- California
- Idaho
- Louisiana

- Nevada
- New Mexico
- Texas
- Washington
- Wisconsin

The remaining states follow equitable distribution rules for property division. I obtained my divorce in New York State which follows equitable distribution of property between the divorcing couple. The goal of the court is to divide property in a fair or equitable manner. Please note this method is not *equal distribution*, but *equitable distribution*, which is not the same thing at all. In equitable distribution the court takes many factors into account to distribute marital property in an effort to arrive at a fair result.

We'll examine those factors in a bit. As we will discuss, things can be complicated.

Starting a Divorce

Divorce proceedings start with a Summons.

Summons with Notice or Summons and Complaint, Followed by an Answer

a. Either a Summons with Notice or a Summons and Complaint are filed with the court to start the lawsuit.

  ii. A divorce is considered a lawsuit where you are suing the other party for a divorce. This is what is referred to as 'filing for divorce'. The Summons notifies the defendant they are being sued for divorce. The Complaint portion of the Summons specifies the filing party's position and reason why a divorce is being pursued.

  iii. Once filed, the court assigns an Index number to your case. The party who files for divorce is the Plaintiff and the receiving spouse is the Defendant.

b. The Defendant is served with the Summons.

c. After being served, the Defendant has three options for response.

  i. File a Verified Answer. The Defendant has a limited amount of time to file a Verified Answer with the court, with a copy to the Plaintiff. The divorce is now contested.

  ii. File an Affidavit of Defendant. The Defendant agrees with the Complaint and the divorce is uncontested.

  iii. Default: no response is given. The law treats each Complaint which is not responded to as uncontested. If a Verified Answer is not completed, a default judgement can be obtained by the Plaintiff, which means the court will approve the divorce on the Plaintiff's terms.

Commencement Date / End Date

When a Summons is filed with the court, a commencement date is automatically established for your divorce and this date is unchangeable. The commencement date is the calendar date that the Summons is filed with the court, through either the Summons with Notice or the Summons and Complaint. It is the start date of your divorce, and also the end date to marital property.

The commencement date becomes crucial in the negotiation stage of divorce. It is used as the end date when calculating equitable distribution. Anything earned by you or your spouse after the commencement date is not considered marital property and is excluded from equitable distribution. Calculations for equitable distribution begin from the date of your marriage through the commencement date of your divorce.

In my case, the Summons was filed in early February, which established the commencement date. I filed the Summons to protect whatever future retirement contributions I made from being included in equitable distribution. Since February was in the middle of a quarterly reporting period, both sides agreed to use the prior December 31st as the end date since it was easier to calculate equitable distribution using recent end-of-year statements. Any monies I contributed to my retirement fund or earned after December 31st would be considered my separate property and excluded from marital property to be divided. Our agreement to use a different end date was for our convenience.

Divorce 101

After the Summons followed by the Answer, the next mandated legal document is the *Stipulation of Settlement*, commonly referred to as the Separation Agreement.

The Separation Agreement details the ending of a marriage in terms of splitting up physical property, assets, debts, current and future payments, and details custody and child support arrangements if children are involved. The Separation Agreement is agreed to by both parties and is reviewed by the court, who ultimately issues a Judgement of Divorce.

That's it. Sounds easy, right? Well, it isn't. Or should I say, not always. The difference lies in the method to get to the Separation Agreement.

Uncontested Divorce

In an uncontested divorce, the spouses come to an agreement on all divorce issues. An uncontested divorce can reduce or even eliminate the need for attorneys. In an uncontested divorce, spouses can:

- handle the legal processes on their own
- cooperate through a mediator
- agree through their individual attorneys to reach a Separation Agreement.

If all issues are agreed upon at the beginning, the Separation Agreement can be filed at the same time as the Summons and Answer.

An uncontested divorce is the most cost-effective method of divorce, which has the added benefit of also reducing the divorce trauma in your life.

Contested Divorce

In a contested divorce, the spouses do not agree. There may be a difference of opinion of what is considered an asset. One or both may feel they deserve more than the equitable distribution calculation. They may need to complete the discovery process to identify what is included. One spouse may be hiding assets or trying to create an unfavorable settlement. For any of these reasons, the divorce can become complicated or combative. The other spouse may be put in a position to protect themselves. In my case, the POS used the divorce process to inflict as much pain as possible and to grab as much money as he could. What an upstanding guy.

In a contested divorce with the Summons/Answer filed, your case is on the court's radar and the court takes an active role in overseeing the progress of the case until a Separation Agreement is reached.

A contested divorce takes more time and money than an uncontested one, sometimes an incredible amount. How much money depends on how much time it takes to reach a settlement, which in turn adds more stress and anxiety to your life.

But hold on, there's more...

The Short and Long of It

The goal in a contested divorce is the same as in an uncontested divorce, which is to file a Separation Agreement.

Getting to the point of a Separation Agreement takes effort. Levels of expectation, cooperation, and reasonableness come into play when negotiating your Separation Agreement, not just between you and your spouse, but also the attorneys.

In an uncontested divorce where you can negotiate with your spouse, a Separation Agreement can be completed relatively quickly, perhaps in weeks or between 2-4 months.

A contested divorce takes longer. Spouses may not agree on anything. They may agree on some points but not on others. If all other points are agreed upon but one issue remains out of agreement, it is still considered a contested divorce.

In my case, the POS contested every issue, which in turn required me to prove every iota of my separate property ownership. My divorce included too much stress, hair-pulling, "I can't believe it!", and "He's claiming what?!" situations. Unfortunately, I was put in the continuous position of defending myself. Although I didn't intend for my divorce journey to be a long, drawn-out event, that's how it ended up.

But hold on, there's more...

Discovery

As you negotiate toward a Separation Agreement, both sides are legally obligated to cooperate in the discovery process. Discovery is a necessary step where each party shares information and provides requested evidence to the other side, which leads to a settlement. This also provides the court access to the facts of the case to make any decisions during the proceedings.

Each side completes a *Statement of Net Worth* which details your financial life. It itemizes how much money you earn, what your monthly expenses are, and what assets and debts you have. It is considered due diligence and is the first step of discovery. It provides detailed information to support your position and hopefully aid your case during negotiations. Let me add that you are required to complete it honestly, something the POS did not feel was necessary.

Attorneys use the *Statement of Net Worth*, in addition to all other discovery documents, as a financial summary of each spouses' income, money, and assets. This due diligence is the foundation for their negotiation strategy and possible trial. Attorneys are also looking for hidden assets and truthfulness in the reporting of assets. In my case, the POS completely lied on his *Statement of Net Worth* and repeatedly did not produce supporting documents or additional discovery documentation as requested. He could not support the false claims on his *Statement of Net Worth*. Eventually these false claims came back to bite him with the Judge which, I believe, ultimately pushed him to negotiate.

Discovery requests can include:

- Request to produce documents (most common)
- Interrogatories: written questions to answer
- Depositions: an interview under oath
- Request for Admissions: admit or deny questions
- Subpoenas

Providing discovery documentation takes time and effort. There may be costs involved from third parties who charge fees for information requested, such as health records, bank statements, retirement fund statements, etc. I spent many nights going through my files, downloading online statements, and making copies for discovery.

You are the best person to gather discovery information and to understand how it relates to your case. Of course, your attorney reviews all documents, and will probably have questions for you to review together prior to presenting to opposing counsel. I was advised by my attorney not to provide any documentation that the POS also had access to, such as a joint bank account, since he had the same access as I did. That saved a small amount of time and effort.

With cooperation from both sides, discovery can move along quickly. On the other hand, if dishonesty, animosity, and anger lead the way, you're in for a long, costly ride, with lots of grief added in.

But hold on, there's more...

Stipulation of Settlement, aka the Separation Agreement

Finally, after all the discovery and negotiation, you have arrived at a Separation Agreement. Great!

The Separation Agreement is your most important document in the divorce process. It is the written contract which outlines the terms you will live with post-divorce. It details how the divorcing couple will divide assets, debts, marital property, and handle custody arrangements and child support. The entire divorce process leads to a Separation Agreement which is agreed to by both parties. It is a binding contract between you and your spouse.

Included in a Separation Agreement are details on distribution related to:

- Real estate: homes
- Assets: cars, household goods, furniture, boats, RVs, jewelry
- Investments: pensions, retirement funds, stocks, bonds
- Financial
    - Assets: savings account, checking account
    - Debts: mortgage, bills, taxes, loans
- Identifies separate property excluded from marital property
- Spousal maintenance (formerly called alimony)
- Child custody, support, and visitation
- Insurance: health insurance, life insurance

Also included are consequences for breach of agreement.

The Separation Agreement usually indicates a timeline for any tasks to be taken directly upon signing. For example, dividing bank accounts or property within 10 days, 30 days, etc.

All immediate disbursements as specified will need to be completed at this point, except for the transfer of retirement funds, which are handled separately via a QDRO (more on that later).

But hold on, there's more…

Trial, The Ultimate Smackdown

If a Separation Agreement cannot be reached after an extended time, you go to trial. A trial is the hardest and most expensive way to resolve your case. The preferred resolution is the divorcing couple settle their differences either working together or through their attorneys.

A very small percentage of cases end in a trial. Most cases are negotiated as you travel along the yellow brick road toward a Separation Agreement. The Judge may encourage negotiation and recommend mediation to resolve the issues between spouses. Settling your case prior to trial is preferred and allows you to have some control over the outcome.

Once you've gotten to trial, you've already spent a tremendous amount of time and money up to that point. The Judge and the attorneys will encourage a settlement up to the very last moment before the start of a trial, and even during the trial itself.

A trial includes submitting documentation, presenting evidence, and calling witnesses. At trial, both attorneys give opening statements, present evidence, and call witnesses. The Plaintiff's side goes first, followed by cross-examination by opposing counsel. The Defendant's side then presents their evidence and witnesses, which the Plaintiff's attorney can cross-examine. All documents and exhibits become part of the official court record. Both attorneys make closing statements to the Judge.

The Judge reviews the facts of the case, applies them to divorce laws and then rules on the issues presented. At this point, the time for negotiation has passed and you are now subject to the Judge's final ruling on the decisions, which is binding. You do not have the opportunity to negotiate the details. The Judge issues a written Judgement of Divorce which takes into consideration all evidence presented at trial. The case is now closed, and you are required to abide by its terms.

In extremely rare situations an appeal of the Judge's decision may be made under certain circumstances based on an incorrect ruling as a matter of law.

But hold on, there's more...

Judgement of Divorce

Once the Separation Agreement is approved by the court, a Judgement of Divorce is issued. The Judgement of Divorce finalizes the divorce process which began with a Summons. It is the legal stamp of approval of the Separation Agreement. Both the Separation Agreement and the Judgement of Divorce are filed in the courts.

The Judgement of Divorce in New York State is typically completed 2-3 months after filing the Separation Agreement.

Divorce processing at court used to be old-school, consisting mainly of hard copy documents and in-person appearances. At the time COVID hit, the courts in my town did not have the infrastructure in place for online divorce processing. The courts shut down and there was nothing to do but wait. The courts eventually reopened but only for limited in-person business, which did not include divorce, causing a tremendous backload in processing divorce paperwork.

My Separation Agreement was only able to be submitted to the court 4 months into the COVID pandemic, 2 months after it was signed. Due to the backload, it took an additional 5 months for the Judgement of Divorce to be issued in December.

I now had a Judgement of Divorce to finalize the divorce process. What a nice Christmas present. Whew, glad that's over.

But hold on, there's more...

QDRO

If the Separation Agreement included a transfer of pension or retirement funds from one spouse to another, that issue is handled in a separate document called a QDRO. A QDRO is a *Qualified Domestic Relations Order.* It is a post-divorce task based on a stipulation agreed to in your Separation Agreement. Consider a QDRO to be a homework assignment to be carried out as outlined in the Separation Agreement but only after the Judgement of Divorce.

A QDRO is a court order issued by the court to move money from one person's pension or retirement fund to a spouse's account. One QDRO is prepared for each account to be divided. If multiple pensions or retirement funds are involved, then multiple QDROs are prepared. You will pay a separate fee for each QDRO.

A QDRO gives the pension fund or retirement plan instructions to transfer the funds. Once retirement monies are transferred, the transfer cannot be reversed or changed except in rare circumstances and only by another court order.

Each individual pension or retirement funds require specific language in the QDRO to move any money. QDROs are not usually prepared by your attorney, but by a separate firm that specializes in the financial language recognized by the fund. Your attorney most probably has a recommendation for a firm which writes QDROs.

Processing a QDRO includes two versions: a draft version and a final version.

Drafting a QDRO

A draft of the QDRO is negotiated and written during the negotiation phase of a divorce and is approved by both spouses. This draft serves several purposes.

- The draft defines the retirement account and amount of money to be transferred which is agreed to by both parties for inclusion into the Separation Agreement.

- The draft is then sent to the retirement fund for their pre-approval. No money is transferred at this time. Pre-approval indicates the retirement fund is agreeable to the language in the QDRO, that no revisions or clarifications are needed, and acknowledges the fund can transfer the money when so ordered by the court.

Details of the drafted QDRO are included in the Separation Agreement. The drafted QDRO is extremely important because it specifies the amount of money in the appropriate legal language necessary for the retirement fund to transfer the money after the Judgement of Divorce is issued. The drafted QDRO usually converts into the final QDRO with no additional changes made.

By getting pre-approval from both the divorcing couple and the retirement fund, the Judge is assured there will be no impediments to executing the transfer of money after the divorce is finalized. This provides confirmation to the court that there would be nothing objectionable by either the spouses or the retirement fund in processing the final QDRO, and no additional legal intervention will be required.

QDRO Calculations

How are calculations for a QDRO determined? The Attorneys gather information during discovery to identify a dollar value of all retirement accounts, IRAs, and pension funds. They will request statements, if available, of each account for both the marriage date and the divorce commencement date, or as close to those dates as possible. In my case, we used the previous end-of-year statements for a mid-February divorce commencement/end date.

The documentation is reviewed to establish what is considered marital property and what is considered separate property. Both sides come to an agreement on the total amount of funds to be transferred from one spouse to another via the QDRO. This is the point in negotiations to claim your separate property if applicable, to be excluded from QDRO calculations. (More on separate property later.)

In general, attorneys start with a 50% split.

Example of QDRO calculation:

Spouse 1 retirement fund:$ 200,000

Spouse 2 retirement fund:$ 100,000

Difference:$ 100,000

Divide difference by 2:$ 50,000

In the above example it has been previously established that both spouse's retirement funds are considered marital property and would be included in QDRO calculations. Each spouse would get equal share of the difference. Spouse 2 would get $50,000 from Spouse 1's retirement funds.

The totals for each would reflect an equal split between the spouses:

- Spouse 1's starting amount of $200,000 is reduced by $50,000 with remaining balance of $150,000.
- Spouse 2's starting amount of $100,000 is increased by $50,000 for a new balance of $150,000.

Please note this is a very simplified example. The $50,000 QDRO transfer above happened to equalize the balance of retirement funds among the spouses. This is assuming an equal 50/50 split is supported to determine marital property. Other factors which can be considered in the calculation of marital property include the date retirement accounts began (pre-marriage) and how the accounts were funded (separate account).

Once the total dollar amount is agreed upon by both parties, that dollar amount is typically converted into a percentage rate. This is the preferred way to handle QDRO calculations and is the most proportional. The percentage rate would be determined for the Spouse transferring the money. In the above example, Spouse 1's total amount to be transferred, 50K, would be converted to a percentage rate of 25% since 50K is 25% of Spouse 1's 200K total. The QDRO would be written to transfer 25% of the balance from Spouse 1's account to Spouse 2.

Using a percentage is preferrable to using a dollar amount because this ensures any market increases or decreases to the accounts are incorporated into the transferred amount. What if the divorce goes on for years? A QDRO is a post-divorce task and can take many months to execute. In the past, divorcing spouses have attempted to postpone executing the QDRO post-divorce in order to keep the money as long as possible. Because of that, both draft and final QDROs have been changed to include clauses which specify: money transfers are required within a certain amount of time post-divorce, and in the case of the receiving spouse's death, the money would be transferred to their estate.

The money is established as no longer belonging to the spouse who is transferring the money but belongs to the spouse receiving the money.

In our example, the QDRO calculations determined that Spouse 2 was to receive a transfer of $50,000 which represented 25% of Spouse 1's total.

Market Increase

To demonstrate why the dollar amount is converted into a percentage rate, let's explore the same example except with a market increase. What if, at the time the QDRO is executed many months, or even years later, market fluctuations have increased the value in Spouse 1's retirement account from $200,000 to $300,000? For ease in calculations, we will assume no change to Spouse 2's account.

Example of QDRO calculation with market increase:

Pre-QDRO transfer:

Spouse 1 retirement fund:$ 300,000 (assume increase from previous $200,000)

Post-QDRO transfer:

Transfer $50,000 flat dollar amount: Spouse 1's account is reduced by $50,000.

Transfer 25% percentage rate: Spouse 1's account is reduced by $75,000.

Using a percentage rate in this example, Spouse 1 paid more money than with a dollar amount.

If you are the person giving the money and the market goes up, you might not like using the percentage rate since it means a higher amount is transferred. But what if the market goes down? It would mean a larger amount of money was transferred from your retirement account than was intended during negotiations.

Market Decrease

L et's explore our example except with a market decrease. What if, at the time the QDRO is executed, market fluctuations decreased the value in Spouse 1's retirement account from $200,000 to $150,000? For ease in calculations, we will again assume no change to Spouse 2's account.

Example of QDRO calculation with market decrease:

Pre-QDRO transfer:

> Spouse 1 retirement fund:$ 150,000 (assume decrease from previous $200,000)

> Post-QDRO transfer:

> Transfer $50,000 flat dollar amount: Spouse 1's account is reduced by $50,000.

> Transfer 25% percentage rate: Spouse 1's account is reduced by $37,500.

Using a percentage rate in this example, Spouse 1 paid less money than with a dollar amount. With a market decrease, the dollar amount of $50,000 represented a greater portion of the account (33%) at time of transfer.

Decreases in account values based on market fluctuations are handled the same way with a percentage rate. If the value of the retirement account goes down, Spouse 2 would receive the appropriate percentage rate based on the decreased market value at the time of transfer.

Percentage Rate

E quitable distribution with a percentage rate does not allow one spouse to claim full gains or losses from market movements. It allows for each spouse to absorb market increases or decreases and ensures a proportional transfer amount.

Using a percentage rate protects both of you.

The money identified in the QDRO is considered the receiving Spouse's money, and therefore they should benefit from any investment gain or claim any loss of that money. By using a percentage rate, the receiving Spouse would receive the appropriate amount based on market value at the time of transfer.

The Final QDRO

The final QDRO is a court order, written and executed after the Judgement of Divorce is issued. The administrators of retirement accounts transfer money only upon receipt of the executed QDRO and not during the negotiation phase of a divorce, or from the drafted QDRO, or upon signing of the Separation Agreement. The final QDRO is a post-divorce task. The retirement account can only transfer money after both the Judgement of Divorce is issued and receipt of the final QDRO. Remember to consider the final QDRO as a homework assignment to be carried out as outlined in the Separation Agreement but only after the Judgement of Divorce.

The Separation Agreement contains the agreement to transfer X amount of retirement money. After the divorce is finalized and a Judgement of Divorce is issued, the final QDRO is written. It includes the details agreed to by both parties in the Separation Agreement and it instructs the retirement fund to complete the money transfer.

Writing the final version of the QDRO does not begin until after the Judgement of Divorce is issued. Prior to starting to write the final QDRO, the QDRO firm requires:

- Copies of applicable pages from the signed Separation Agreement. This ensures that all points outlined in the drafted QDRO are included in the final QDRO.
- A copy of the Judgement of Divorce, which authorizes them to write the final version.

Once written, the final version is forwarded to both spouses for review and signature. After their signatures, it is then filed with the court for the Judge's signature.

The final QDRO when signed by the Judge serves two purposes:

- It is recorded along with the Separation Agreement and Judgement of Divorce as proof that the legalities of the agreed-upon money transfer are completed. Executing the post-divorce QDRO typically completes the divorce paperwork with the courts.

- A certified copy of the court order is requested, usually by the recipient's counsel, and forwarded to the retirement fund. This certified copy of the fully executed QDRO is required by the retirement fund to complete the transfer of money, which can take up to 120 days.

QDRO Timeline

QDRO Firm:	Drafts the QDRO, with account details and amount of money for transfer, usually a percentage rate.
Spouses:	Review and agree to the drafted QDRO.
Retirement Fund:	Pre-approves the drafted QDRO.
Separation Agreement:	Filed with the court, including details of the drafted QDRO
Judgement of Divorce:	Issued by the court. The divorce is now finalized.
QDRO firm:	Writes final QDRO after receiving copies of Separation Agreement and Judgement of Divorce.
Spouses:	Sign final QDRO, which is then filed with the court.
Judge:	Signs final QDRO, which is filed along with the Judgement of Divorce.
Certified Copy final QDRO:	Usually requested by receiving spouse's counsel, is sent to the retirement fund.
Retirement fund:	Receives certified copy of final QDRO and transfers the money.

But hold on, there's more...

QDRO Retainer

The retainer you originally signed with your lawyer ends upon the Judgement of Divorce. Since details of the QDRO are included in your Separation Agreement, the drafted QDRO is part of your original retainer with your attorney. The retainer does not extend to post-divorce tasks such as the final QDRO.

As the QDRO is a post-divorce task, you are required to sign a separate QDRO retainer if you wish to have legal representation for the final QDRO.

However, you are not required to sign a QDRO retainer with the same divorce lawyer who represented you for your Separation Agreement through to Judgement of Divorce. You are free to either stay with the same attorney or choose a different attorney. You also do not need to have legal representation at all for the QDRO and have the option of representing yourself.

There is no additional negotiation at this point since everything has already been negotiated, agreed to, and detailed in the Separation Agreement. I did not sign a separate QDRO retainer with my attorney, but instead chose to represent myself. I contacted both the QDRO firm and opposing counsel directly to advise them I was representing myself for the final QDRO and all related matters should be addressed to me.

My QDRO was straightforward. It included a flat percentage rate of my annuity account to be transferred to my now ex-husband. Since the details of my QDRO were not complicated, I was comfortable handling the final QDRO myself. I did research on what to include in a QDRO, mistakes typically made, and read samples of completed QDROs.

I provided the QDRO firm with the requested documentation from the Separation Agreement and Judgement of Divorce. Upon completion, the final QDRO was then sent to both opposing counsel and myself for review. I compared the details in the Separation Agreement against the final QDRO for completeness. My review of the final QDRO identified several minor typographical errors for correction, and even requested one additional point of compliance which was not included in the Separation Agreement, but I had identified from my research. Opposing counsel did not dispute my changes or have any additional recommendations. The final QDRO was signed by the POS and I, and then forwarded to the court.

After the Judge's signature, I called opposing counsel to confirm that a certified copy of the signed QDRO was forwarded to the retirement fund to complete the money transfer. With that follow up, my legal obligations were fulfilled, and all the post-divorce tasks were now completed.

I expect that most people sign a QDRO retainer and continue to use their divorce attorney for this final divorce-related legal issue. It is probably easier that way. Due to the relative simplicity of my QDRO, I was happy with my choice to handle it myself. The estimated savings from attorney fees was approximately $3,000. Good for me!

In my case it worked out that I handled the QDRO myself but don't be hesitant to use an attorney. The QDRO has immediate effects on your retirement account. Once the money is transferred by court order, it cannot be undone unless by a second court order, which is highly unlikely.

So that's it. Easy, right?

Key Take-Aways:

Step 1: Summons/Answer

Step 2: Discovery

Step 3: Negotiation (Good luck!)

Step 4: Separation Agreement

Step 5: Perform tasks as outlined in the Separation Agreement, i.e. distribution of property, bank accounts, etc. Distribution of pension/retirement funds are handled separately with a QDRO.

Step 6: A trial if a Separation Agreement cannot be reached.

Step 7: The court issues a Judgement of Divorce.

Step 8: Final QDRO submitted to the court for Judge's signature.

Step 9: QDRO with Judge's signature is filed with other divorce documents.

Step 10: A certified copy of the fully executed QDRO is forwarded to the retirement fund for transfer.

Step 11: The retirement fund transfers the money.

Step 12: You've reached the end, time to celebrate.

Chapter 3:
Let's Talk
Equitable Distribution

Is your state an equitable distribution state? In divorce equitable distribution means both parties share everything acquired during the marriage, both assets and debts. My recent divorce was in New York which is an equitable distribution state.

The court uses the term equitable distribution. Equitable distribution is the division of property, assets, and debts between spouses during divorce. The division of property can be through a separation agreement, a property settlement, or by judicial decree. Equitable distribution is determined on a case-by-case basis, subject to negotiation between the two parties and at the discretion of the Judge.

Equitable distribution does not necessarily mean dividing down the middle. With equitable distribution the court attempts to divide marital property fairly. Taken into consideration are assets, debts, financial contributions to the marriage, future needs, and how long the marriage lasted. Other factors such as future employability and earning power are also considered. The aim is to divide assets equitably, which is not the same as equally.

It's a hard concept to accept. Emotional aspects of divorce leak into financial negotiations. Human nature does not want the other side to get as much. In a divorce reasoning and emotions often blur together during negotiation.

Equitable distribution means your future ex-spouse gets a portion of what you built throughout your marriage, regardless of:

- how your spouse is acting in the divorce
- your spouse's maturity
- your spouse's character
- if they lied
- if they are a jerk
- how mad you are at them
- how mad they are at you
- if they don't deserve it
- how unfair it would be

If you were wronged, it's natural to want justice. Except you need to understand one major point, which is that justice has *no part* in your divorce case. The basis of your case centers around the law of equitable distribution regarding marital property. It's a money transaction. That's it. That's everything.

The sooner you start thinking in terms of sharing property and assets, the smoother your divorce will be. That's how the Judge is required to think about it. When you recognize that, you will cut down the time to get to a Separation Agreement and save money. Money which is better in your pocket than your attorney's.

Separate Property

Separate property is excluded from equitable distribution calculations in a divorce. Separate property, also called non-marital property, includes property: owned by you prior to your marriage received as a gift or inheritance during the marriage acquired during the marriage with separate funds

If you have separate property, any income derived from it is also considered separate. However, if any of that property or income money is co-mingled with marital funds, it could be considered marital property.

Any payments for separate property should be paid from separate funds, such as from an individual bank account funded by your paychecks, and not from marital funds. Keeping the money separate ensures the property remains separate. If payments for separate property come out of a marital account, that property could no longer be considered separate but is included in marital assets for equitable distribution. A good financial management plan for couples is where each have separate money as well as a joint account. Money can be transferred from your individual account to a joint account for shared marital expenses.

Upon filing a Summons/Answer with the court, the filing date is the commencement date of the divorce which is used at the end date in calculations. Any financial gains or losses for equitable distribution calculations end with the commencement date.

If a Summons/Answer has not been filed with the court and will be filed along with the Separation Agreement, the commencement date of the divorce would be the date both documents are jointly filed. Any financial gains or losses from financial investments remain as marital property up until that joint filing date.

Learn what may qualify as separate property in your case so you can include any eligible separate property claims in equitable distribution discussions. It may help you protect your assets where you can, and also to determine the validity of what your spouse is claiming as their separate property.

Include all your separate property in your equitable distribution negotiations, even if you don't have immediate proof. The attorneys may accept it as part of equitable distribution calculations while you continue to research for proof.

In my case I was able to prove separate property on a portion of my retirement funds, which saved a good amount from being included in equitable distribution. Of course, the POS didn't like that one bit.

Key Take-Aways:

Equitable distribution does not mean equal distribution.

Keep payments and income for separate property financially separate from marital finances.

What qualifies as separate property in your case?

Include all separate property in calculations even if you cannot immediately prove it.

Continue your research to get proof.

Entitlement is a wonderful thing.

Chapter 4:
Divorce Strategy

Which divorce strategy is right for you?

People are unpredictable. Divorce often brings out buried emotions and unrecognizable actions by your spouse. Maybe the emotions are not so buried after all, but closer to the surface, as hurt and anger often are. When money is involved, it only gets worse. Greed is the ultimate motivator. Can you anticipate which way your divorce will go, whether amicable or cut-throat? Or somewhere in between? Unfortunately, since there are two of you in this divorce, it's not entirely in your control. More accurately, I should say there are four of you in your divorce, including the attorneys. That's four people whose actions and decisions will resolve your future, not just you.

The divorce process is the same whether it includes court oversight or not. There is only one process for attorneys to follow: discovery, followed by either negotiation to a Separation Agreement, or a trial. Different experiences in reaching the end goal lie in what method is used.

Outlined are how I categorize the different strategies to divorce.

Option 1: Mediation

The first option is to go to a mediator. The mediator meets with both spouses at the same time to educate the divorcing couple on requirements of a Separation Agreement and guides them to a decision on the issues. The mediator's job is to define the terms of the Separation Agreement which would be acceptable to the court, where both you and your spouse agree on all details. This includes everything that is typically included in a Separation Agreement, such as assets, debts, house, car, retirement, child custody, and child support, etc.

In an uncontested divorce, both the Summons/Answer and the Separation Agreement can be filed with the court at the same time by the mediator.

In my first divorce, we saw the mediator only four times. The first time he advised us what issues should be included in the Separation Agreement. The second and third time we discussed details and came to an agreement for each issue. The fourth time was to sign the Separation Agreement which was filed along with the Summons/Answer.

The legal aspect went quickly. Of course, there is always emotional recovery and healing afterwards, but the legal aspect was smooth. Having recently been through an extended divorce from hell, I can appreciate the simplicity of the least traumatic strategy experienced with my first divorce.

This option is a strategy which required both parties to be mindful of the goal and can reach an agreement.

Option 2: To Each His Own, but Let's Negotiate

The second option is for the divorcing couple to each get their own attorney. The attorneys assist with hashing out the details of the Separation Agreement.

That is not to say that the appropriate due diligence for discovery is skipped or that negotiation is absent from this option. Discovery is very much a part of divorce for all divorce strategies and is the foundation for negotiations between the divorcing couple. Inevitably there may be some differences of opinion or heated moments during the negotiations, but ultimately an agreement is reached.

The timeline for this strategy can be either long or short, depending upon how long it takes the divorcing couple (and their respective attorneys) to negotiate their way to a Separation Agreement. The legal aspect consists of either filing the Separation Agreement along with the Summons/Answer, or filing the Summons/Answer first, followed by a Separation Agreement at a later date.

This strategy can work when both parties are still somewhat rational and are mindful of achieving the final goal. Some accord between the divorcing couple exists, even if it is just to arrive at a Separation Agreement.

Option 3: To Each His Own, Going-for-the-Jugular

Remember that the goal of divorce is to get out alive. Achieving that goal would be helped by getting to a Separation Agreement sooner rather than later, addressing all divorce details without taking many months, or even years. Sadly, that is not always achievable. Your spouse may have a different view on how to proceed. Mine did.

The third option is similar to option #2 where each spouse gets their own attorney, but with a major difference because one or both spouses go for the jugular. They may be unwilling to compromise, feel they deserve more of the marital property, disagree with the concept of equitable distribution, or purposely use the divorce process to vent their anger and punish their spouse. Every issue becomes contentious, and their agenda consists of fighting dirty any way they could, even to the extent of stupidity.

Some of the many ways to have a contentious divorce:

- Partial or no compliance with the discovery process
- Exaggeration or outright lying on court documents
- Extended legal maneuvers
- Filing unnecessary motions before the court
- An inability to come to an agreement
- Blind insistence that they deserve more, more, and more
- The people who benefit most from this strategy are the attorneys.

In a contested divorce with the Summons/Answer filed, your case is on the court's radar and the court takes an active role in overseeing the progress of the case until a Separation Agreement is reached. Discovery and negotiation can move along and then stutter repeatedly while the divorcing couple fails to arrive at a Separation Agreement. There are regular court appearances for both parties along with their attorneys for periodic check-ins with the court. In my case once the Summons and Complaint was filed the clock began with court oversight.

Although not of my choosing, my divorce fit into the going-for-the-jugular approach. I had been through an amicable divorce and was more than open to reaching an agreement, although my spouse had no such intention.

In my case, the POS could not seem to contain himself. His rage was ultimate, massive, intense, and laser focused on me. If he could have destroyed me and left me destitute, he would have, without question. He went after everything of mine, whether it originated before our marriage or not. Both he and his Barracuda attorney refused to negotiate. The general expectation of both seemed to be they hit the jackpot and would walk away with buckets of money. Both played dirty, outright lied, and used every mean, nasty trick they could throughout the proceedings. Their only agenda was to go-for-the-jugular. I was in a street fight, plain and simple, fighting for survival and paying for the privilege.

So how do you survive a Going-for-the-Jugular divorce?

Just like playing a game of Deal or No Deal, you make the best decision with the board you have on each round of play. At the end of the game, you see how it could have been played differently had you only known what was in each suitcase, or what was revealed in the next round of play.

However, there is strategy to the process and learning from other's past experiences. People often get greedy for a larger amount and end up losing most of it.

A reasonable strategy is the best way to achieve a more positive result.

Option 4: In Comes a Trial, Out Goes Money

The goal of each of the options previously discussed is to reach a reasonable Separation Agreement. After a Separation Agreement is filed, it is approved by the court and a Judgement of Divorce is issued.

Regardless of any motions filed with the court, or negotiations toward a Separation Agreement, attorneys follow the same process. If a Separation Agreement cannot be achieved, you ultimately end in trial, where the Judge makes final decisions for both of you.

The endpoint of filing a Summons/Answer with the court is a divorce trial. That is not the preferred endpoint, but it is the last stop on the yellow brick road of divorce. If opposing sides cannot agree, the divorce goes to trial where the Judge decides upon the issues based upon the facts presented. At that point, neither spouse has a voice regarding arriving at the decisions. There is no negotiation with the court, and the court's verdicts are final.

The court would rather the divorcing couple reach their own settlement without going to trial. The spouses are actively encouraged by the court to work it out, and the attorneys are encouraged to negotiate the issues. The court may instruct the divorcing couple to go to mediation to resolve their issues.

In my situation, we were not making headway and the negotiations were dragging out for months. At one court appearance, the Judge instructed us to go into a private room to negotiate. Another time, the Judge took the bench to formally speak to us about our case. Not to the attorneys, but to myself as the Plaintiff and my estranged spouse as the Defendant. Just like you see on television, we sat at the respective Plaintiff and Defendant tables in the courtroom along with our attorneys and were sworn in.

The Judge implored us to negotiate and find our way to a Separation Agreement, and not to leave the personal decisions of our divorce up to him. To quote him "This is not a case which needs to go to trial. I'm begging you to speak to one another, or through your attorneys, to come to an agreement.

You do not want me making these decisions for you." I completely agreed with the Judge and encouraged my attorney to speak to opposing counsel. I was scared to speak directly to the POS. He would have considered it a sign of weakness and would have twisted anything I said.

You are advised to communicate through your attorney, which is what I did. I can't say whether going through my attorney helped the divorce more or less since both the POS and the Barracuda were out for blood and not inclined to make anything easier. In hindsight I should have tried speaking to the POS directly, futile though it would have been.

A Separation Agreement is preferable all-around to a divorce trial. Trial is too expensive. My attorney's standard retainer fee to *start* to prepare for trial was $25,000. Of course, that retainer would quickly disintegrate while the trial clock kept ticking. I cannot even begin to imagine how many attorney hours would be required for a full trial.

At trial, the Judge makes the decisions based on the evidence presented by the attorneys. What evidence? Whatever you can prove.

Key Take-Aways:

Divorce is when you'll see someone's true character.

How they behave speaks to their core goodness, or lack thereof.

How nasty is your spouse?

Going to trial is the same as flushing your money down the toilet.

Which strategy will be used in your divorce?

Encourage a negotiation strategy.

Make the best of a bad situation.

Chapter 5:
Lawyers Do What Lawyers Do

Your lawyer's responsibility is to bring your case through the legal process, hopefully looking out for your best interests along the way. That is how it's supposed to work. But while guiding your case through the legal process what if every decision by your attorney is not in your best interest? Moving your case through the legal process and your best interests are two separate goals which do not necessarily co-exist.

The atmosphere in the courthouse is unhurried and hushed. For court appearances, you sign in and then wait for your case to be called. You wait outside while the attorneys answer questions in the Judge's chambers. You wait again for the next court date to be assigned. There is no hurry, no sense of urgency. Your lawyer takes your case through the legal paces, all in due time.

Regular court appearances were part of my case and I saw how attorneys interact with the court. As a divorce attorney they spend a lot of time at the court and regularly work with the Judges, their clerks, and the court employees. Of course, they want to look good in their dealings at court. Contrary to what you've seen in the movies, lawyers do not grandstand in the courtroom. You will not see big, dramatic displays of lawyering. It would be bad form and not well received. Is every legal decision for your case based on your best outcome, or perhaps a decision is made because your attorney doesn't wish to rock the boat at court?

Although your lawyer takes you through the legal process, you are the person ultimately looking out for your interests. Understand where you are coming from and what your goals are vs. where your attorney is coming from and what their goals are. You and your attorney may have different perspectives.

For example:

- Your expectation may be to get to a Separation Agreement within 4-5 months.

- Your attorney's expectation may be to get to a Separation Agreement in due time, with no particular rush. "Please understand these things take time."

Obviously, these are different perspectives with different timeframes. So, which works best for you? Granted, the Judge guides both the court appearances and discussions in chambers with the attorneys, but it doesn't hurt to have a game plan. What is the plan in between the court appearances? Talk to your attorney about aligning your individual perspectives, and your expectations.

Choosing a Lawyer

You need a lawyer, so how do you choose one? The short answer is it's a crap shoot.

Lawyers are intimidating. The whole divorce process is intimidating, especially while you are upset or anxious. My hope in writing of my experience is it will help to reduce some of that intimidation. Choosing a lawyer is hard and the average person cannot determine if a lawyer is good or bad. How would you know? Either someone gave you their name as a reference, or you did an internet search for nearby lawyers.

As you step into the world of divorce, interview a few attorneys. Take your time with this part of the process and do your own due diligence. In most instances there is no immediate rush and an extra 2-3 weeks would not make too much of a difference in your case. You are in no rush to find an attorney and do not need to pick the first one who you meet with.

When speaking to a potential attorney, it's ok to ask them some tough questions. You need to ask them questions. Remember that you are interviewing them to see who is best for your case. They are not interviewing you. How they respond to your questions is critical.

Here are some questions to ask when choosing an attorney:

- What are their strengths?
- How good are they at negotiation?
- How many of their cases have gone to trial?
- How long is their average time between retainer and separation agreement?
- How committed are they to reaching an agreement?
- What strategies do they use to negotiate?
- What is their estimated cost of a motion?
- Can you reach them after hours?

I chose my attorney because she told me she was an excellent negotiator, which I knew I would badly need. As it turned out, I didn't see any great negotiating skills. She did, however, negotiate with *me* to accept whatever opposing counsel was offering even if it was not in my best interests. Of course, had I agreed it would have made her job a whole lot easier, but I learned I had to push back so that she would in turn push back on opposing counsel. I felt she didn't want to rock the boat or call the opposing side out on their behavior. The POS would have taken her strategy as weakness to be capitalized on, and increased his demands repeatedly.

I observed that attorneys have a way of not responding to a direct question. Perhaps they take a course in law school on evasive discussion. Avoidance is a strategy in itself. My lawyer had this ability and used it in her conversations with me, which I did not appreciate.

How invested is your attorney in your case? How available are they? My attorney changed law firms without any advance warning three weeks after I signed the retainer. As the client, she could have shown respect and advised me what was going on. As the case progressed, I also found out there was no way to contact her outside of regular Monday through Friday business hours. While it is understandable a lawyer may not wish to give clients their cell phone number, there should be some way to contact them, perhaps through an answering service, when an emergency arises. My attorney provided no ability to contact her outside of regular business hours and repeatedly avoided the question when I inquired. For that reason alone, I should have changed attorneys. She was not as invested as I was.

Dissatisfied with your attorney? You have the right to change your attorney at any time. If you are unhappy with how your case is being handled, you can choose a new attorney to represent you. Similarly, your attorney can also end their representation of your case. Your retainer probably details this possibility, such as timeframe, notifications, and access to case documentation. If either party chooses to end your business relationship, appropriate papers are filed with the court to reflect the change of attorney status. Speak to your attorney if you have concerns and then make your decision. Are they respectful of what is concerning to you, and act appropriately?

Don't be afraid of changing your attorney. It is an option available to you if you don't agree with the way your case is being handled. You can remove your attorney from your case even if you do not have a replacement attorney yet. Papers would be filed with the court that your attorney is no longer representing you. When you get a new attorney, they will file a document with the court that they are now representing your case.

If that is the case, don't be afraid of making a change. You would need to sign a retainer with the new attorney. You'll pay attorney fees for your case whether it is to your old attorney or to a new one. A new attorney brings a new perspective to the case.

In my case the thought to get a new attorney crossed my mind several times and I should have acted on it.

I highly recommend you take a step back at intervals throughout your divorce process and examine how your attorney is handling your case. Sometimes it's just not a good fit.

What Lawyers Are Not

In discussing lawyers, first let's recognize what your lawyer is not.

Your lawyer is not your therapist. Perhaps your spouse was a miserable husband or wife, lied to you or cheated on you. Okay. You may need to unload those emotions, but they do not belong in discussions with your attorney unless they relate to a point of law.

Your lawyer is also not your friend. They are not overly concerned with saying you were wronged by your spouse. Their purpose is not to hold your hand or commiserate with you. They don't care if your estranged spouse gave you an attitude or was rude. Your lawyer will be happy to listen to you complain about what your spouse did, how mean they were, and how they don't deserve anything. Be aware that those minutes of complaint can turn into hours which then add up to considerable attorney fees. Is this how you want to spend your money? Probably not.

Get a therapist, talk to friends, join an online group, or start a journal. All are good choices to unload some stress and emotions. Heck, I'll come over and listen to you vent at a reduced rate of only $400 per hour. Although it may make you feel better in the short term, it doesn't do you case or your wallet any good to unload your emotions or complain about your spouse to your attorney. It does not help your legal situation, and only adds more debt to your financial situation.

Obviously if there are serious safety issues involving law enforcement or an *Order of Protection*, such as physical abuse or an unsafe situation which could change your case, you need to bring it to your attorney's attention. In my case there was one incident where I felt I needed to call the police because the POS was having a meltdown over food in the refrigerator (of all things!) and was screaming so loudly at me that he became hoarse. He was out of control to the point I felt unsafe and called 911. It was the right thing to do. I waited in my car for the police to arrive, and then filed a report against him. Of course, he seemed to calm down when speaking to the police when they arrived. The experience must have made an impression on him or else his lawyer must have advised him to change his behavior because after that he kept to himself, which was a small benefit to me. The experience highlighted his extreme emotional swings and how he felt entitled to act out. It made me more nervous in my own home.

Do your best to keep the discussions with your attorney on points regarding your case. It will help your divorce continue to move forward.

What Lawyers Are

Your lawyer has experience with the ebb and flow of processing a divorce case, while I assume you do not. A divorce is new territory for you, or, like me, a contested divorce is new territory. You are at a disadvantage here and need help to navigate a process which can be smooth or messy, depending upon the situation and the participants.

Your lawyer is performing a service for you. They advise you regarding decisions for your case. They handle the intricacies of discovery, negotiations, legal documents and court process. Understanding the legal options is crucial. Your lawyer provides the necessary explanations and guidance to the many options available along the way. They guide you through the legal strategies for your case and represent you in court.

The Yellow Brick Road

Lawyers follow the one legal path allowed to them. They go through the paces of the legal system, submit the legal paperwork, represent you in negotiations and before the court.

Lawyers present the issues and options to you, but as the client, the decisions are ultimately yours to make, and the decisions are not easy. You are making important legal decisions without knowledge or experience while working through intense emotions. Lawyers are happy to explain all the necessary details and provide guidance at their hourly rate. The cost is $.

Similar to what Dorothy experienced on the yellow brick road, the path forward is not as simple as it first appears. Complications begin, and every single word, document, and action is reviewed, commented on, judged, and debated with your attorney, the opposing side, or the court, while the bills continue to build. The continued cost is $$.

The path of divorce ends with a trial. As it was explained to me, we prepare for trial while pursuing a settlement. Preparing for trial takes mountains of paperwork, a great deal of time, and is ridiculously expensive. Think $$$.

As you move along the yellow brick road trying to get to the Wizard for a Judgement of Divorce, be aware of ways you can save yourself time and money.

The Wrong Path

Is your case proceeding the way you want? How motivated is your attorney to negotiate a settlement? Take a minute to think about it and ask questions if appropriate. Your questions will either confirm you are on the correct path or identify the need for a change. A change which may save you more money in the long run.

Several times I felt my attorney did not represent something correctly or a mistake was made regarding strategy. Instead of pursuing the issue, I talked myself out of it by thinking "she knows best" or "she knows what she's doing."

Wrong. I was very wrong. I should have trusted my instincts and questioned her further. I should have called her on it and requested a change in strategy or pivoted down a different path.

Or hired a new attorney.

And if any of your family or friends suggest that you may want to change attorneys, listen to them! They can see from the outside what you may not be able to clearly see from the inside.

Then get a new attorney.

Key Take-Aways:

Your lawyer is not your therapist.

A therapist costs a lot less than an attorney.

Your lawyer is not your friend.

They are performing a service for you.

Stick to the issues and discuss the progress of your case.

Do you agree with how the case is proceeding?

Have they been less than upfront?

Are they getting results?

Discuss it with them or think about making a change.

Don't be afraid of change.

Chapter 6:
Now That You Have a Lawyer

Paperwork Supports Your Case

You know the saying that the most important thing in real estate is location, location, location? Well, the most important thing in divorce is documentation, documentation, documentation.

Before anything, lawyers need facts. Lots and lots of facts and specific details, which are only valid if you can provide supporting documentation.

How much is your home worth? Did you own it before marriage? Who paid the mortgage? Who is on the deed? What bank account was the check from 20 years ago written against? Do you have copies of the checks? Who bought this or that? Where did the money come from? Did you share a bank account? How much is your monthly utility bill? What do you spend on food? Did you recently repaint the house? What did it cost? Any home improvements? How long ago? Who paid for it? How old is your car? How much do you spend on clothing? Do you have a retirement account? How much is in it? When did you start it? How much was it worth when you were married? Are any assets pre-marital?

The answer to all the above questions, and any others, is...can you prove it?

Your lawyer needs all these facts to understand the strength of your case, the strength of the opposing side, where your case stands now, the extent of the agreement to be reached, and next steps. The court needs the facts to oversee the processing of your case and to instruct the parties on how to proceed.

I stated earlier that the court's interest is to distribute assets equitably. That's the law. Notice I did not say fair distribution, because fair is questionable. The court uses the term 'equitable', but that is not always the reality. Without documentation to the contrary, your spouse can get as much as half. Based on your specific situation, that may not be fair. Mine sure wasn't.

How do you prove anything? With documentation. Your word is one thing, but documentation is proof. Keep any paperwork regarding your assets at the time of your marriage. It doesn't matter if you are married for 10, 20, 30 years, you may need it. Keep the paperwork both from your pre-marital life as well as documentation from your married life. Better yet, keep all paperwork from before, during and after your marriage. Documentation doesn't expire so keep it forever.

If you think you will be able to go back to a company or bank for paperwork, you may not have much luck there. Banks and other financial companies do not keep records indefinitely. At most, they keep 7 years' worth. Maybe you'll find one rare company that keeps 10 years, but never more than that. Many companies have had multiple computer upgrades over the years and getting any historical data is questionable at best. Still, other companies may have changed their name or been merged, not just once, but various times over the years, and the data is unavailable or gone. It will take time and effort to track everything down, with very questionable results. How much easier it would be to save your own paperwork. If you don't wish to keep monthly statements, then at least keep end-of-year statements.

Banks and institutions offer recent digital statements accessed via your online accounts. Companies do not keep years of historical records visible on their website. You may be able to see your statements online for only a limited amount of time, perhaps within the last year or two at the most.

I recommend you go into your online accounts and download your statements while they are still viewable. Email them to yourself to keep indefinitely in digital format. If you have older paper copies you wish to get rid of, take a picture of each and email them to yourself for a digital record.

It's up to you to keep your own documentation to protect yourself. You may need it to prove what you never expected to prove and to protect yourself from the one person you never thought you would need to protect yourself from. Better to err on the side of caution.

So, what paperwork do you need?

Example Paperwork

Marriage License

Prenuptial agreement if applicable

For House:

- Who is legal owner?
- Deed, mortgage(s), statements, balance
- Appraisal or value of the house at time of purchase
- Appraisal or value of the house at time of marriage
- Appraisal or value of the house at commencement/end date
- Total spent on home improvements plus receipts
- Who paid for improvements?
- What account were payments made from?

For Rental:

- Rental agreement
- Rental insurance policy

For Car:

- Title, car insurance policy
- Loan statement and balance
- Was car purchased before or during marriage?
- How much was the car?
- What account were payments made from?

Pension/Retirement Funds:

- Plan information
- Annuity statements
- What date did the account start?
- What was the account value at the date of the marriage?

- What is the account value at commencement/end date?
- How was the account funded?

Life Insurance:

- Policy, with beneficiaries
- Statements
- When did the policy begin?
- What account were payments made from?

Assets:

- Bank statements, at least yearly
- Credit union statements
- What was the value at the date of the marriage?
- What is the current value?
- How was asset funded?

Debts:

- Credit card statements
- Loan contracts, payment schedule, balance

Ongoing Expenses:

- Utilities, food, clothing, gas, etc.

Educational degree, if applicable:

- Starting date
- Ending date
- Where did funds come from?

Medical Records, if applicable:

- Past 2-5 years

How You Can Help Your Case

It's all about the documentation.

Start with your own and gather whatever paperwork you can to help prove your case. Most law firms have either another attorney on staff or an outside financial specialist to perform a financial review of discovery documentation, both yours and from the opposing side. Your attorney needs to understand what the assets are. The cost for this financial review is in addition to your attorney's review. In my case, my attorney passed documentation to another in-house counsel who specialized in financial review. His hourly rate was the same as my attorney's rate. You are paying twice for review of financial documentation for your case.

Organizing your paperwork before presenting it to your attorney will help to reduce billable hours. Don't just throw all your papers into one pile. It would be easier to understand, and ultimately less costly to you, to sort and separate your paperwork by category. For example, your house documents in one folder, car documents in another folder, insurance in another folder, and so on. Then sort each folder's documents by date. The time spent will save you time and money in the long run. If your documents are submitted to your attorney in a clear manner, it will reduce the confusion and cost to you.

After you've finished with your paperwork, move onto the documentation submitted by your spouse. Do your own review of their documents. Write down any questions you may have. Are there holes in the timeline? Was money transferred? Where did it originate from? Where was it transferred to? Identify the gaps, make your attorney aware, and request clarification in the form of additional discovery.

In my case, the POS provided very little as part of discovery. He submitted a spreadsheet from his business with no supporting documentation, his credit card statements, and a portion of his business bank statements. We requested bank statements for gaps of time which had conveniently been omitted from discovery. We also asked for documentation to support his business deductions, which we never got. The POS and opposing counsel had no problem either partially responding to discovery requests, or simply not responding at all. I started to repeat the words "forensic accountant" to my attorney for her to use in conversation with opposing counsel, which probably helped to push them toward negotiation, however slowly.

If the opposing side does not freely provide their discovery documentation, do not get sidetracked by opposing counsel. In my case, the Barracuda used every nasty trick to avoid submitting discovery documents, including: sending the same inadequate/partial documents again, flat out ignoring continued requests, reprimanding our side for causing them distress by our discovery requests, and twisting the conversation to attack our side for daring to ask for discovery.

Don't fall for these or similar underhanded tactics which are designed to take the focus off the request. You are entitled to any and all documents for discovery. Push your attorney to get all discovery requests fulfilled as quickly as possible by whatever legal means available. This is not the time to be hesitant. It will save you time and money in the long run.

In my case, we couldn't seem to get past the discovery stage. We went through multiple court appearances asking for discovery. If the opposing side is not forthcoming with discovery documents, my recommendation is to send subpoenas to whatever companies, banks, or funds as necessary to get the information you need. The information the subpoenas provide far outweighs the costs and will be far less than the cost of attorneys back and forth emails, or the cost of court appearances during the delays. It will save you not just money, but time as well. Do it!

Separate Property Claim

If you have any separate property claims, present them as clearly as possible along with any supporting documentation.

In my case I had pre-marital retirement money which had been transferred several times over the years until landing in its' current account. My attorney and I tried to review these retirement assets but following the money trail was confusing, not only to my attorney, but initially to me as well since details were forgotten over the years.

Because the assets were related to retirement, I had kept my paperwork. I thought perhaps one day I may need to prove the retirement money to the IRS for tax purposes. As it turned out, I needed it to prove origination, ownership, and historical transfers as part of my divorce. Since I obviously knew the history better than anyone, I told my attorney to stop reviewing the retirement funds, and that I would provide a clear timeline with supporting documentation for my separate property claim. I didn't need to pay for work which I was better suited to complete.

I was claiming this money as separate property and intended to prove it. Prior to negotiation I dragged out all my paperwork to prepare my claim. It took quite a bit of time to sort through my documents and create a timeline, which I continued to revise over the next few weeks as various facts were confirmed or remembered.

With my documentation I was able to prove the start, middle, and endpoint of my retirement funds. My documentation helped to support my separate property claim and exclude those funds from marital property considered for equitable distribution.

For my purposes, presenting the timeline of the retirement funds in an organized grid was preferable than verbal explanations. I believe that a clear grid presents information in an easy-to-understand format and eliminates confusion. I submitted copies of the timeline with attached supporting documentation to both attorneys at our in-person negotiation session. It was invaluable to support my claim.

A copy of the grid I developed is included for your reference. Modify it as needed for your situation. Or use it to understand the documentation your spouse is claiming as separate property, to ensure the documentation they submitted is complete and accurate.

Sample Timeline of Pre-Marital Retirement Funds

Amount at Opening	Plan Manager	Opening Date	Account Owner	Account Number	Closed Date	Amount at Rollover	Rollover Date	Rollover Account #	Notes

In retirement accounts, pre-marital money plus any earned interest from that account remains pre-marital property in a divorce if you can prove that no marital funds contributed to the current balance. That was good for me, and ultimately saved that money from being included for equitable distribution.

My detailed timeline saved many billable hours' worth of review from both my attorney and the financial specialist. Since I would have had to review their draft and make appropriate corrections, it was easier for me to create it from scratch myself. Doing that work saved me countless hours of legal fees. My effort = saved $$$.

If you don't have documentation or a way to provide a separate property claim, a 50% split is usually the starting point for equitable distribution of assets accrued during the marriage. If you cannot prove partial or full ownership prior to your marriage, then it is on the table for distribution between the spouses. Do whatever research you can to determine the timeline for any funds that may be separate property. Reach out to associated financial institutions which manage any separate property accounts for any documentation to help support your claim.

By the way, during negotiations, opposing counsel did not question the timeline or the total amount of retirement funds I was claiming as separate property. I was not asked even one question by either my attorney or opposing counsel to further clarify the information I was presenting. The entire amount of my claim was accepted and therefore deducted dollar-for-dollar from marital distribution. My total was taken right off the top. Seeing it in a clear format with supporting documentation solidified my claim and eliminated any counter argument against it.

Stay Focused on the Goal

Understand that your estranged spouse's past actions do not exclude them from equitable distribution. Fair has nothing to do with it. You may feel your spouse is not entitled to any distribution, or less distribution, but recognize the law starts with the theory that both parties get something, whether you like it or not. The spouse always gets something, that's how it plays out in court unless you can prove otherwise. It's a hard concept which may not sit well in your heart or your brain. But you need to stay focused and get to a place of acceptance of that concept. The sooner you do, the sooner negotiations can begin. Move the process along and get to a reasonable Separation Agreement.

I wrote earlier that lawyers have the experience on the ebb and flow of a divorce case, which is true. What is not clear is how motivated a lawyer is to expedite the completion of your case. Remember that is the goal – to expedite your case to the best obtainable resolution.

Please notice that nowhere have I said it would be a fair resolution or that justice will be served. I said the best obtainable resolution. Unfortunately, there are limited methods to achieve that goal. Both you and your attorney have no choice but to follow the divorce process. Focus on the goal and move it along as best you can, even if that means pushing your attorney along as well.

I should correct that statement: YOUR goal is to expedite your case to the best obtainable resolution. Your lawyer's goal may be different. How hard does your lawyer attempt to come to an agreement without trial? What specific actions has your lawyer done to get to a negotiation table? Have they written opposing counsel, or phoned them? How many times? How recently? What is your lawyer's timeline to getting to an agreement in your case? What constraints are preventing or stopping negotiations, and what can be done to move past them?

I would ask your lawyer on a regular basis what is being done to negotiate toward a settlement. Don't be afraid to ask. Believe me when I tell you it will save you money in the long run. Listen to what their plan is as well as their timeline and respond accordingly.

And if they don't have a plan? That says it all.

Check Emotions at the Door

All divorce cases have similarities. While lawyers can provide guidance on your case as it progresses, on all the legal implications and strategies, they cannot address the toll it takes on you.

Lawyers deal with the legal details, which is their job. However, the details are many, and of course, arguable. Your discussions and the divorce process will move along better if you can keep your emotions out of it, which is admittedly hard to do. Try your best to take a detached approach. Anything that helps keep your focus on the goal will have the positive side-effect of lowering both your blood pressure and your attorney fees.

On a personal level, the contentious nature of the POS was already a major source of anxiety to me. The constant attack by opposing counsel was another front to defend and fight against, adding further stress onto my shoulders. It was a long, extended period of unrelenting stress with no reprieve in sight. The personal attacks by opposing counsel got to the point that I inquired of my attorney how I could make a formal complaint of harassment to the court. As it turned out, I didn't get the chance to follow through with that since we were informed shortly after that the POS had changed attorneys.

So, What Do You Want?

What do you want to get out of the negotiations? Sit down and decide what are your primary goals.

Make a list and give it to your attorney. Does your list seem reasonable? Does your attorney feel it is reasonable? Are your goals obtainable in your specific case? How confident is your attorney that they can secure these goals in your Separation Agreement? Bear in mind the court will also be looking at the Separation Agreement for reasonableness.

Write down your priorities so both you and your attorney can use it as a guide in negotiations. Perhaps break down your list into low, medium, and high priorities. Keep it nearby as reference and to help retain your focus as you negotiate along the road to a Separation Agreement.

Fees are Up, Up, and Away

What is opposing council's approach with a client like my husband, who wants to go after everything? Who resists every effort at negotiation and goes for the jugular? It's Christmas for them. They can request a mountain of documents, rack up a mountain of billable hours reviewing those documents, write a mountain of emails to your attorney requesting various clarifications, and so on. And that means your attorney will also rack up a mountain of billable hours reading through the mountain of documents and emails.

There are so many options to discuss, clarify, consider, then decide. It's a bit confusing and you need to go through it again? No problem. Want to clarify something, or need an explanation of how the process works? Sure thing. There are too many short discussions which turn into long discussions which adds up very quickly into big money.

Sometimes your lawyer will tell you a story from a previous case which may have a similarity to yours. While interesting, that 5-10 minutes will cost you money. Is that story worth $150-$200 to you? I was extremely vigilant about keeping the conversation on track and cut my lawyer off when she went off topic, but it still added up like crazy. All those extended discussions on strategy build up your bill, in addition to court appearance fees including attorney's parking fees, which by the way, you also pay for.

I saw first-hand how quickly telephone conversations with my attorney could add up. After a few months, I employed tactics to reduce telephone time and save money. I started to announce an end time to our calls, "I have to hang up in 15 minutes, where do we stand and what is the next step?". I found it to be a very effective technique to keep the conversation focused and reduce costs. Before hanging up I would also state how long the call lasted, which avoided misunderstandings, "Our call was 15 minutes long." You could even keep a journal on the duration of your calls to reconcile against your monthly bill.

I'm here to tell you that, yes, this can go on indefinitely. Much longer than you think is even possible. Don't fool yourself into believing it will be over in 2 months, 4 months, or 6 months. More questions, more requests, more documents, more billable hours. The whole thing goes around and around, like a hamster running endlessly on a wheel. Except you are the hamster, getting nowhere fast and paying for it all.

Positive/Negative

Your lawyer assists you through the legal process. That statement is both a positive and a negative. Positive because your attorney knows the inner workings of divorce and you are getting the legal guidance you need. Negative because lawyers have no alternative to the current process which takes time. Divorce does not move along quickly. There are many detours along the yellow brick road. It can become a long, drawn-out marathon event instead of a short or even medium length sprint. Do anything you can to move the process along.

Time for a New One?

More than once, I considered getting a new attorney. Two things held me back. One was the money I estimated it would cost to pay another attorney to get up to speed on the case. Was that the right decision? It's hard to definitively say, but upon reflection I would say no, it was not the right decision. Money was flying out the door and I was scared it would be even more money going out the door. Moving to a different attorney, even allowing for up-front costs, would probably have cost less money in the long run by saving time in getting to a Separation Agreement sooner. I probably over-estimated the cost of changing attorneys and should have investigated the real cost of getting a new attorney instead of projecting what turnover cost would be.

The second reason was I was overwhelmed. The thought of finding a new lawyer was too difficult. At the time, having to search for another attorney was too much to deal with. The point of least resistance was to maintain the status quo with my current attorney. That was a mistake, and I should have pushed through those hesitations and fears.

As the case was progressing, two people commented to me that maybe I should consider a new lawyer. I didn't want to hear it, but they were right. My recommendation when people offer this advice is to listen. Listen and act on it. An outsider is seeing and hearing the case from a detached perspective, can see what you can't or what you don't want to admit.

Looking back, I should have gotten a new attorney.

Divorce is a cooperative path travelled by you and your attorney. It can be hard to know when to be directed by your attorney and when to push back. Several times in my case I was a strong guiding hand in the process, more so than I felt my attorney was. Those were the times I achieved successes along the way and there were other times I should have spoken up more. I regret letting some things slide and not speaking up.

Shakespeare Knew What He Was Talking About

I am reminded of the William Shakespeare quote from *King Henry VI, Part 2*: "The first thing we do, let's kill all the lawyers".

Do you need a lawyer for your divorce? Yes. But Lawyers also complicate and unnecessarily extend the process. Perhaps I'm being unfair since divorce itself is a complicated and messy process. My case was small potatoes compared to others and should have been more easily negotiated, even allowing for the POS's sheer insanity. I guided my attorney toward certain strategies, where I felt it was my attorney's place to strategize regarding the best way to move forward and guide my case accordingly, even with both a hostile opposing counsel and hostile claimant.

My expectation was for my lawyer to know how to move it along at a better pace. Isn't that part of their job? Not just to be on the defensive. I felt that my attorney was complacent to the process instead of guiding the path we should take.

Buyer beware. Get the assistance you need, even if that assistance is a new attorney.

Key Take-Aways:

Paperwork doesn't expire.

Help your case where possible.

Figure out if you have any separate property claims.

What can you prove?

Review your spouse's separate property claims.

Stay focused.

Figure out what you want.

Write it down for your attorney.

Is your lawyer developing strategy?

Why not?

You can get a new attorney.

Chapter 7:
Court Appearances

Court appearances continue until either a Separation Agreement is signed, or a trial begins. Before you leave each court appearance, your case is assigned the next court date. Once scheduled on the court's calendar, it is generally not changed. And while it may be rescheduled, the court does not skip a court appearance.

Court cases are made up of an unbelievable amount of discussion and paperwork with your attorney. Discussions on the purpose of the paperwork, the options, where each option can lead, your response, their potential response, the court's potential response, and so on.

Once the Summons/Answer is filed with the court, follow-up court appearances are required to provide the court with an update on how the case is progressing. Court appearances are mandatory for both parties along with their attorneys. In my case, we were required to appear before the court every six weeks to report on our progress.

I liked the Judge on my case. I felt he was a good Judge and trying to be fair. Understand that "fair" does not mean the Judge will side with you. Although you may feel it is unfair for the other party to get something, the Judge does not see it that way. He cannot see it that way and is required by law to divide assets – some to you and some to your spouse. You'll have to get your mind around the concept that your spouse will get something. Resisting that basic truth will only compound your aggravation and extend negotiations.

I had court appearances every 6 weeks for a year. During that time there were two instances where the Judge spoke to us directly to encourage negotiation. All other court appearances were handled by the attorneys, while spouses waited in the hallway.

During court appearances (pre-Covid), all parties were required to be at the court by 9:00 am. The lawyers check in with the court officer. All parties must be present to be acknowledged on the court's docket and then you wait until your case is called. When called, the attorneys joined the Judge in chambers while the claimants wait outside. The Judge guides the conversation with the attorneys, questions them regarding the progress of the case, gives decisions on any issues and instructs on next steps. Your lawyer speaks on your behalf and will update you regarding the conversation as well as any instructions from the court. You are not permitted to speak to the Judge.

Court appearances are intimidating. You are not privy to what is happening and look to your attorney to explain what happened and interpret its meaning. The Court keeps the process moving along the track to trial.

In my case, each court appearance took approximately 3 to 4 hours, which, if you are keeping count, was about $2,000 each.

Key Take-Aways:

Bring quarters for the parking meters at court.

There's a whole lot of not talking going on in court.

Has there been any movement on the case?

What's happening in the Judge's chambers?

What does it mean to my case?

This is taking too long.

It seems like nothing is happening.

When is the next appearance?

How much did this cost?

Chapter 8:
Subpoenas

What is a Subpoena?

A subpoena is a court ordered command requiring some action, either to appear in court, or to produce documents for evidence.

There are two common types of subpoenas:

- Subpoena ad testificandum: which orders a person to testify in court

- Subpoena duces tecum: which orders a person or organization to present physical evidence to the court, usually a request for documents.

Subpoenas can be used to require documentation from a person, bank, retirement plan, or business for evidence to support your case.

My Experience

In my divorce, I discovered that the POS did whatever he could to remove money and secure assets from various accounts prior to the start of the divorce process. He: withdrew all the money out of a retirement plan, removed me as beneficiary to his life insurance policy, and removed my access to his business bank account.

The court does not condone such actions and looks unfavorably upon the person who performs those types of financial maneuvers. During divorce proceedings all financial interests of the spouses are to remain intact. Existing accounts are to remain unchanged. Everything is part of equitable distribution until it is determined otherwise. Neither spouse has the prerogative to hide any finances prior to the divorce or at any point in the divorce process as you negotiate toward a Separation Agreement. Both parties are expected to be honest in their financial representation. Financial maneuvering pre – or post-commencement of divorce, although not strictly illegal, demonstrates underhanded tactics and does not conform to the premise of equitable distribution used by many states, including New York State.

I told my attorney what I discovered and asked for subpoenas to get documented proof. Her response was "Subpoenas are usually for trial. We don't do that at this point."

What? Wait for trial? Aren't we hoping to avoid trial? Wait to get proof of the POS's dirty maneuvers? Absolutely not, let's get it now. My attorney's recommendation seemed like a backwards strategy to me. I completely disagreed and said as much to her. When I asked how much a subpoena cost and was told $500 each, I asked for the subpoenas to be issued immediately, by the end of the day. I provided her with company name and account details and the subpoenas were sent that day. It was a good value for the money and worth the cost. I firmly believed getting proof of his financial maneuvers would add weight to our argument in negotiations. Why would I want to wait for trial? Looking back, her inability to see the strategy was ample reason to get a new attorney.

A subpoena gives the recipient 30 days' notice to provide the requested documentation. In my case, the timing was perfect. Responses to the subpoenas were received around the time an emergency motion was submitted by my spouse's Barracuda attorney. The subpoena responses were included as evidence in our response to the court based on the emergency motion and was acknowledged by the Judge in his ruling.

Asking for subpoenas was the single best decision I made in my case, and they were absolutely worth every penny. The subpoenas were unimpeachable proof of underhanded tactics by my spouse and were key tools to give strength to my legal argument.

Key Take-Aways:

Don't wait to send subpoenas.

They can be powerful tools to discover what is going on.

This documented proof can be used in negotiations.

Chapter 9:
Motions

What is a Motion?

A motion is a request to the court to decide on a specific issue.

A motion has three parts, all of which are filed with the court:

- a motion

- a response,

- and a counter-response.

When a claimant files a motion, the other party submits a response, and the original claimant can submit a final counter-response.

- Side A files a motion

- Side B submits their response to the motion

- Side A submits a final counter-response

The Judge reviews all three parts of the motion then presents their decision on the issues included in the motion. The court's response to a motion is received in writing, not at a court appearance. It takes weeks to get the response, which your attorney will probably email to you.

An emergency motion requests an immediate response from the Judge, with a mandatory appearance before the court within two days, regardless of the date of your next regularly scheduled court appearance.

Types of Motions

Motions can be:

- A Temporary Order, requested while the divorce case is pending, such as a:
  - ○ Temporary custody order
  - ○ Temporary restraining order
  - ○ Temporary exclusive use of marital residence
  - ○ Temporary attorney fees payments
  - ○ Temporary support payments
  - ○ Temporary order prohibiting use of marital assets
- A Request for Adjournment: for a court appearance or court date
- A Motion to Dismiss: requesting case to be dismissed prior to trial
- A Motion for Discovery: to compel compliance with discovery process

In general, a motion before the court will cost approximately $15,000 in legal fees for each side. That includes at least one court appearance, discussions with your attorney, gathering facts or evidence for your response, determining strategy, drafting and submitting your response, reviewing the counter-response, analysis of the court's decision and its' impact on your case. From start to finish a motion takes months to complete.

If you are submitting the motion, do you feel the court will respond in your favor? And will the response gain you more than $15,000?

My Experience

In my case the Barracuda filed an emergency motion at 3:00 pm on a Friday in May just before the court closed for the day. With an emergency motion, the court is required to immediately revise their docket to accommodate the emergency issue and mandates an interim court appearance within 2 business days of the emergency motion.

We were directed to appear in court within the 2-day guideline on the following Tuesday even though our regular court appearance was scheduled four business days away on Thursday of the same week.

The emergency motion in my case consisted of four issues:

- The first issue regarded a change to the health insurance plan he was receiving through my employment from my new job.

- Payment of his car insurance.

- The POS requested payment for all attorney fees incurred both to-date plus all future fees with the argument that he could not afford it, while I could. In his motion the POS *demanded* (yes, demanded!) the Judge order me to pay him $25,000 immediately upon execution of the motion, plus all future attorney fees for the duration of the divorce proceedings.

- The last request was for interim maintenance (previously known as alimony). Interim maintenance payments apply only during divorce proceedings and end upon the Judgement of Divorce. The POS requested interim maintenance based on false total income listed on his *Statement of Net Worth*. He was trying to establish the need for interim maintenance as a prelude to his request-ing permanent alimony in the separation agreement. If interim maintenance were awarded, it would set a precedent for him to receive long term or permanent maintenance. It was an obvious money grab and ludicrous in the extreme. The POS was basing his demands on the lies he presented in his *Statement of Net Worth*.

I'm sure the POS and his attorney thought they were being so clever and strategic in filing the emergency motion. But to the contrary, the Judge seemed irritated by it. By law the Judge had to rearrange his docket to include our case within two days, and we met on the following Tuesday. While speaking to the attorneys in his chambers during our emergency court appearance, the Judge advised opposing counsel that this was not a true emergency motion and could have waited until the next regularly scheduled court appearance which was scheduled for two days away on Thursday. Not a good start for the other side, and an obvious power play.

Health Insurance

The Judge had one immediate issue with the motion which was the matter of health insurance. The Judge instructed us to go into a private conference room to work it out. He would consider the other issues included in the emergency motion but wanted us to resolve the health insurance issue. That is where I first felt that my attorney, the self-proclaimed great negotiator, was not so great at negotiating after all.

Included in the motion was the opposing side's objection to my upcoming job change, which would change my health insurance coverage as a result. Since the POS was included on my health insurance policy through my employer, his health insurance would change as well. What a thing I had to deal with while switching jobs.

I had come to court prepared with a listing of the POS's doctors. I had called each doctor's office and was able to get confirmation that 8 out of 9 of his physicians accepted the new insurance plan, except for his primary physician. I have to say the Barracuda lived up to her name and came on strong in the conference room. She was intense, rude, and confrontational. She made the argument that since it was his primary physician, his very life was in jeopardy, and he was dependent upon this doctor to keep him alive. All very dramatic but an absolute crock. In the conference room, we went back and forth on this issue for quite a while.

My attorney and I stepped outside the conference room for a minute to discuss it, and my lawyer suggested I pay COBRA for the POS for the duration of the divorce proceedings. When I questioned how long it would be, I was advised only a "few months." With no other options, I agreed since we were under pressure from the Judge to resolve this health insurance issue. I truly believed it would be over in a few months. Unbelievably, the few months turned into 18 months at a cost of over $20,000 due to how long it took to negotiate to a Separation Agreement and to get a divorce decree in COVID time.

In my case, it would have been better to negotiate a specific term for COBRA payments, perhaps for 6 months or through the end of the year. I'm angry with my attorney, who should have known better. She should have suggested adding a concrete end date to the stipulation, instead of leaving the payments open-ended until the Judgement of Divorce. For goodness sakes, was this the first time my attorney made an agreement like this? She should have known better and protected me. I ended up unnecessarily paying the POS's COBRA for 18 months while the insurance from my new employer was excellent.

My paying COBRA was a terrible waste of money. It meant nothing to her that I had to write out that check every month. There was no urgency on her part to resolve the case as it lingered on and on through negotiations, the Separation Agreement, and delays to the final Judgement of Divorce. Remember my previous comment that perhaps attorney's behavior was shaped by how they wish to be perceived in court and not necessarily in the best interests of their client? I felt my attorney steamrolled me into agreeing to this stipulation because it was expedient for the emergency motion even though it was not in my best interest. I cannot say if it was the only solution the Judge would have agreed to, but we should have pursued other options or at least negotiated for an end date. My attorney did not earn her money that day. On the contrary, she cost me money. Lots of it.

Emergency Motion and Subpoena Responses

Back to the emergency motion. We were asked by the Judge to resolve only the health insurance issue on that day. After we reported the resolution of that issue to the Judge, we were free to leave the courthouse. The next step was to prepare and file a formal written response to the remaining issues included in the emergency motion.

The POS claimed in his motion that I had disregard for his health, which I rebutted in my response with specific examples where I scheduled and attended his doctor's appointments, picked up his monthly prescriptions, and processed insurance paperwork for him.

Our written response pushed back against the request for alimony and attorney fees as having no basis. We pointed out incompleteness in my spouse's financial statements presented as discovery in addition to inaccuracies in his *Statement of Net Worth*. We presented that my spouse had stopped paying his share of bills in the house while continuing to live there and highlighted obviously suspicious expense claims in his *Statement of Net Worth*.

Remember the subpoenas I made my attorney file? The responses to be subpoenas were received just prior to the date the emergency motion was filed. The emergency motion gave us the platform to advise the Judge of the responses to the subpoenas. Specifically, the POS had withdrawn all assets from his only retirement annuity to hide marital funds. He had also removed me as a beneficiary to his life insurance and removed my access to his business account.

As we've discussed, these actions are prohibited in a divorce proceeding. All financial accounts of either party are considered marital property until determined otherwise and are to remain unchanged during divorce proceedings as you work toward a Separation Agreement. I was able to present documented proof to the court that the POS had engaged in pre-divorce manipulation of marital funds for his own benefit, and the court agreed.

Incidentally, in their final counter-response to the emergency motion, the POS and Barracuda did not respond at all regarding his financial maneuverings. Not one word regarding withdrawing over 60K from his annuity. Which was to be expected since what could he possibly say to justify his actions?

The Court's Response

After the emergency court appearance, our filing a response and the opposing side's filing of their counter-response, we waited for the Judge's written response which arrived weeks later. By that time, it was over three months from the initial date of the emergency motion.

I was very fearful to read the court's response. How could I afford to pay if any more of the motion issues went in his favor? The scared feeling in the pit of my stomach turned into a full-blown meltdown as I started to read the Judge's response. I was hyperventilating while anticipating what the response would be. I thought I was going to have a heart attack, or faint, or both. Is this what a heart attack feels like? At that moment I was more scared over my physical reaction than continuing to read the Judge's response. I realized I was having a panic attack, and wow, was that scary.

As I started to read, I began to breathe again.

Car Insurance

On the matter of car insurance, the Judge observed that since the POS had started non-payment of bills, which, at the time, was approximately $500 per month, he had the means to the pay for his own car insurance, which was considerably less at $80 per month.

The request for car insurance payments in the motion was denied.

What kind of man is so petty to put a motion before the court over $80 a month? Well, now we know.

By the way, it was just the beginning of his underhanded tactic to stop payments. After that he stopped all payments outright.

Attorney Fees

On the matter of attorney fees, the Judge may not have appreciated the "demand" in the motion instructing him to rule a certain way.

In his response the Judge noted that the POS had money to pay his attorney more up to that point than I had paid my attorney up to that point, which demonstrated his ability to pay was no less than my ability to pay.

The request of my paying his attorney fees was denied.

Interim Maintenance (Alimony)

On the matter of interim maintenance, previously known as alimony, the court uses a worksheet, applying a formula as a guide whether to give alimony and how much to give.

The POS submitted ONE single piece of paper to the court to substantiate his income. It was a spreadsheet from his business, which I know was fudged. No other corroborating documentation was provided. His business income was compared against my salaried income, which is like comparing oranges to apples. The court's formula used his net income from his business after all expenses were deducted whereas it was compared to my gross income. I did not have the advantage of having my expenses deducted. It was an extremely lopsided comparison when in reality his income was more than mine.

In our motion response, we argued that the POS had stopped contributing financially to bills. His claims of spending $2,000 per month on food, $795 per month to charity, and $250 per month to online gambling (!) were not to be considered as legitimate expenses toward calculations in the worksheet. Who spends $2,000 per month on food for one person? Is he eating lobster and caviar every day? He was also claiming he needed interim maintenance (alimony) from me because he was giving his money to charity and spending it on gambling. His argument was that I should compensate his charity and online gambling. Absurd.

I knew the POS would say anything to further his own cause. While I am not surprised of his lies, I don't understand how the Barracuda allowed such flamboyant, obviously false claims on an official *Statement of Net Worth* submitted before the court. Didn't she question his lies, or did she knowingly submit a false document to the court? Absolutely they were both in on it.

In the court's response, the worksheet calculations were not given much credibility. The Judge pointed out that since the POS was still living in my house, he had no immediate need for interim alimony. The Judge also noted the POS's counter-response included no explanation of his pre-divorce financial maneuverings.

The interim maintenance issue was denied.

Written Response

The court acknowledged copies of the subpoena responses attached to our emergency motion response which demonstrated the POS had engaged in pre-divorce financial maneuvering, which is not regarded favorably. The Judge rightly concluded that the POS did not have "clean hands." Clean hands is a legal term indicating the claimant engaged in wrongdoing and unfair conduct and, as a result, their claims are jeopardized or invalidated. The Judge saw through the POS' deceptive behavior and denied his claims.

The court's response:

1. COBRA was previously agreed to, and the health insurance issue is resolved.

2. Response to car insurance was denied.

3. Response to payment of attorney fees was denied.

4. Response to interim alimony was denied.

Denied, denied, denied.

Grateful me. ((::happy dance::))

In Summary

Overall, the court's response to the motion was favorable to me. I was grateful the Judge was able to see through the bogus claims the POS presented in the emergency motion. Grateful that the truth was visible through the lies and the court's decisions were made based on facts.

The POS thought he was so smart, but it worked against him in the end. The Judge rightly saw through his money grab while the emergency motion gave me the platform to bring his underhanded actions to the court's attention.

I would have liked to hear the subsequent conversations between the Barracuda and the POS regarding the court's response, along with the Barracuda's explanations. To say the POS would have disagreed with the response is an understatement. He wouldn't have taken it well at all and probably flipped out. Being told by the Judge you do not have clean hands must be shocking, to say the least. It speaks to your character, which the court determined to be lacking. You've been found out. Perhaps you, dear reader, or I, would be embarrassed, but not the POS. His personality is such that whatever he talked himself into believing was the gospel truth and everyone else should completely agree and recognize that as well. I'm sure he was shocked the Judge didn't believe his lies.

My lawyer explained that the court's responses for a motion very often set the tone for what the court's rulings would be at trial. It gives insight to which way the court would be inclined to respond in trial. Luckily, I was able to give my attorney ammunition for the motion response. All I did was shine light on his underhanded maneuverings, which worked in my favor. That's a bit of justice. Good for me, for finding out what he did and pushing my attorney to send the subpoenas and get proof. Good for the Judge, for recognizing underhanded tactics were used.

The court's response to the emergency motion was a milestone in the proceedings. It must have hit the POS and his Barracuda lawyer right between the eyes. The Barracuda did not come through for him. They were expecting a big pot of gold at the end of the rainbow, but instead they were woken up as to the reality of their claims. As a result, it must have become apparent that their side did not have nearly as strong a case as originally thought.

The response absolutely caused dissention between the POS and his Barracuda attorney, because soon after we received word that the Barracuda was no longer representing the case, and a new attorney was taking over. Perhaps the Barracuda saw how their demands to the Judge failed and did not wish to appear before the court with either questionable evidence or a questionable client. My attorney felt the court's response to the motion was the deciding factor for the Barracuda to step back. It was either that or else the POS fired his attorney because she did not produce the response he was promised. So sad.

Now, the Barracuda was out, and a new attorney was in. Interesting, but would it help my case?

Key Take-Aways:

A motion to the court costs lots of money.

An emergency motion does not always represent a true emergency.

Change in plans, report to the court.

Prepare as best you can.

Listen to the court's instructions.

Is your attorney working in your best interest?

Put a calendar end date on any stipulations!!

Review opposing documentation and question anything suspicious.

Help your case by getting subpoenas to prove questionable behavior.

Gather documentation to present the opposing side's lies.

Present all arguments in your response.

Chapter 10:
Out with the Old,
In with the New

In my case, my husband's first lawyer would not entertain the possibility of negotiating to reach an agreement. It was apparent to both my attorney and I that the Barracuda was taking her cues from the POS. He was vicious; therefore, his attorney was vicious, and their combined stance was hardline from the start. The Barracuda did not maintain an attorney's impartial attitude or even pretend to. It was full attack mode at every opportunity and every email, discussion, and court appearance was contentious throughout the entire process. The anger from the Barracuda was palpable. Where was an attorney's impartial demeanor? It got so bad that I asked my attorney how to make a formal complaint to the court about her harassing behavior. But before I could act upon that, my attorney received notice that a new attorney was representing the case. It was just after the motion response. So, the Barracuda was now out. My attorney's guess was she dropped her representation when it became apparent their case was not a slam-dunk as originally thought. Or perhaps she didn't want to represent a client who did not have "clean hands".

We met the new attorney during the next court appearance. When I walked in, my attorney was sitting in the second row of the gallery, and I joined her. In the first row was a man who was standing and leaning over his briefcase, searching for something. I couldn't see his face clearly.

After I sat down, my attorney and I started to talk. I commented that considering the court's response to the motion, hopefully this new opposing counsel would explain realistic options to his client, and we could start to negotiate. My attorney and I continued to comment on the case. I don't remember specifics of our discussion after that, and although it wasn't too deep into the details of our case, it was a private conversation.

Court is not a place for loud conversation, and we were speaking softly. The man in the front row continued to search around in his briefcase for the entirety of our conversation, which seemed odd because his search was so prolonged. I looked at him again and instantly recognized him as the new attorney on the case. I leaned forward and said to the man "Aren't you Mr. X?" He made a great show of acting surprised that we were there. Oh, please. He knew who we were and was purposely spying on our conversation. He had set it up. How very ethical of him. Okay, so now we know who we are dealing with.

Of course, we couldn't take back what was said. Although he heard us, in hindsight I think it was good to encourage the opposing side toward negotiation as the only path through this mess. They really had no choice since things weren't going their way, and I'm sure the money was running out.

As expected during that court appearance, the two attorneys were called into the judge's chambers. The new attorney claimed he couldn't speak regarding details because he was getting acclimated to the case. My attorney requested discovery documents which were not provided by the previous opposing counsel. The Judge advised them to continue with discovery. That's it. That's the total of what happened. No worries, since it only cost $1,750. Gulp.

Key Take-Aways:

Court appearances cost money.

Court appearances take several hours.

Careful not to be overheard while in court.

I see you, Mr. Opposing Counsel.

How long can this be dragged out for?

What's next?

Chapter 11:
Negotiations

Greed

It was obvious the POS was out for blood and intended to get it. And that meant money. He went after everything. Never mind that he came into the marriage not just penniless, but heavily in debt with $50,000 owed in back taxes, a wallet full of maxed out charge cards, and not one cent to his name. It didn't matter that I helped him out financially upon our marriage, he went after every penny in the divorce and didn't leave anything out. He didn't care what position it would put me in, if it would force me to sell the house which I owned for more than 15 years prior to our marriage, or if it would make me destitute. There was no pretense of appreciation for past assistance, no sense of fair play, no respect for the years of our marriage, or the tremendous financial help he received from me.

The POS felt tremendously entitled to everything I ever had without regard if it was pre-marital. His greed was monumental and all-encompassing. He just wanted it all and would have taken it without any remorse and without looking back. If he could have left me homeless and penniless, he would have, and then patted himself on the back. In his mind, all his actions were justified.

And because he was in attack mode, I was required to defend my whole life. He was on the offensive, and I was absolutely on the defensive. I had to prove ownership of everything, and if I couldn't prove previous ownership, it was on the table for him to get half. While I was proving my life, he also proved many things. He proved his lack of character. He proved his lack of integrity. He proved his lack of ethics. And he proved his lack of morality.

The POS fought every single truth, used every underhanded trick, outright lied in his court documents, and did anything it took to take what wasn't his. He spent two to three times the amount of money on attorney fees than he received in the settlement. His greed cost him more than it was worth. It was a very poor return on his investment. What an idiot.

Unfortunately, I was put in the position of having to spend big money to save myself from an idiot.

Hindsight Hurts

I didn't have a pre-nuptial agreement for my second marriage. Boy, was that the wrong move. I trusted him and believed it when he swore to me "On my honor as a man I would never do that to you." What a joke! Stupid, gullible me. He sounded so sincere that I believed him. I was wrong on a monumental scale. What was monumental was his anger. His greed was stronger than his vow. His promises meant nothing, and his actions spoke far louder than any words, current or previous.

I naively thought a marriage was where you look out for and help each other. Where a promise to your spouse has meaning and value. Where even if things don't work out, you have some small degree of respect for the time you were together in the marriage and part ways with a drop of integrity. Silly me.

Fair? Of course not. But who said anything about fair? Divorce is not about fairness.

Hindsight is 20-20. I regret being stupid and not protecting myself better. It was a terribly hard lesson to learn. All I could do at this point was minimize the fallout the best I was able to.

Try, Try Again

The Barracuda was not inclined to negotiate. All efforts were rejected. Do I think my attorney could have tried harder to negotiate with her? Absolutely. Do I also think the POS and Barracuda would have continued to turn it down?

Absolutely. Mine was a particularly nasty divorce, but that doesn't mean you shouldn't try. It doesn't mean everyone would react that way, or that your spouse and opposing counsel would. Continue your efforts to get opposing side to a negotiation table. What is rejected at first may be reconsidered after three months, six months, or a year, and it's worth the attempt. Perhaps once opposing side experiences large sums of money going down the toilet, they'll have a change of heart.

Would you rather negotiate $50,000 in a settlement or give $75,000 to your attorney to get a $25,000 settlement?

Getting to the Table

During multiple court appearances, we continued to ask for discovery documentation from the opposing side. The Judge was not pleased we continued to be stuck in the same place with no forward progress made. During the second court appearance with new opposing counsel, the Judge repeated his instructions to produce discovery documents, advising my attorney to also send the court a copy of our itemized discovery list. The Judge was pushing the opposing side to follow court procedure and comply with discovery.

My guess is that the new opposing counsel stalled as long as possible because additional discovery documents would reflect poorly on his client, whose character was already in question with the court.

Our discovery letter requested the POS provide documentation:

- To support claims on his Statement of Net Worth of $2,000 per month on food, $795 per month to charity, and $250 per month in online gambling fees. (So obviously false, did he think these expenses would be blindly accepted?)
- Of $60,000 he withdrew from his annuity, which was conveniently excluded from prior discovery documents.
- Of all statements from a PayPal account, also conveniently excluded from both personal and business discovery documents.
- Of all statements to support claims of his business expenses.

I'm sure our discovery requests were not well received, and it's no wonder they were stalling. The POS was so arrogant he believed he could go after me for everything, and he wouldn't need to provide his own documentation.

I pushed my attorney to file a Motion for Discovery, but she felt it would look bad before the Judge since his response to the emergency motion was in my favor. She felt it would be bad form. I didn't agree but deferred to her judgement and waited for their response to our requests. That was a mistake on my part. I should have insisted. I expect it would have moved negotiations along faster.

When hired onto this case, opposing counsel inherited quite a situation. The court had denied the previous attorney's motion partly based on proof that his client acted improperly and did not have clean hands. Now his client was non-compliant in the discovery phase. Opposing counsel was specifically instructed by the Judge to produce documents which would most probably negatively reflect on his client, as well as highlight suspicious statements filed with the court. Perhaps his client's business documentation would also raise questions. Not an ideal situation to be in. I imagine opposing counsel didn't want to take the chance. Attorneys do not wish to appear lacking or present their client in a bad light in front of the Judge.

I suspect opposing counsel was open to the idea of negotiation sooner than his client. The POS held out in the misguided certainty he was right and would be rewarded for his bogus claims and outright lies. I believe he continued to hang on until his money ran out. Sometimes it takes quite a while until you realize you're stupid. Negotiations started over one year (!) after divorce proceedings began. Unbelievably, it still took five months, plus multiple court appearances and plenty of emails, to get to a negotiation table after his new counsel was assigned to his case.

In-person negotiation was scheduled for early March of year 2 at my attorney's office.

Prepare

Prepare yourself for negotiations as best as you can. Beforehand, think of what you want for reasonable property distribution and financial arrangements. Discuss it with your attorney and be clear what your expectations are.

How I also prepared was to read "The Art of the Deal" by Donald Trump, which is not about divorce at all, but helped me think in terms of negotiating toward the end goal.

From an internet search I came across a good article which breaks down negotiation tactics, "How to Use & Diffuse Hardball Tactics in Negotiating" by Max Factor III. It's worth reading.

The Negotiation Table

Lawyers are supposed to be logical and unemotional during negotiation, and for the most part they are. They tell you options, you discuss strategy, and they speak for you. My lawyer was businesslike for the most part, however, I did see her emotions surface during negotiation, which happened at the very worst time.

By the time negotiations came around, I was so stressed and anxious that I asked my attorney if I could remain in an adjoining office. I couldn't bring myself to sit at the table and listen to the opposing side sling their crap. It was too overwhelming for me. I wanted to protect myself from all the hate thrown my way and instead wanted to hear just the boiled-down offer, so I stayed in an adjoining room while my attorney went into the negotiation room.

My impression was that my attorney seemed to hear the opposing side's requests and then try to negotiate with *me* to accept their offer, instead of negotiating with *them* to reduce their requests. I did not see evidence of the fantastic negotiation skills my attorney claimed to have when I retained her. I felt I had to prove my points first to her before she would take them to opposing counsel, and sometimes I had to insist. How much easier would her job have been if I just agreed to everything the opposing side presented in their initial offer?

During the first break in negotiations, she excitedly came into the room to say, "This could all go away right now!". Very dramatic, but please give me details. She relayed an offer which covered 4 or 5 points. Was that it? Where were the other 8 or 9 points? There were big, huge gaps of unaddressed issues missing. As she relayed the offer, I wrote the details down on a homemade grid I had drawn which allowed me to immediately see what issues still needed to be addressed. When I asked about the remaining issues, she had a blank look on her face and no answers.

This wasn't going well, in my opinion. Or hers either, I bet. She was most definitely annoyed by my questions and sighed dramatically when I rejected the offer as incomplete. Apparently, I was supposed to jump into the air and immediately agree to whatever the offer was. Instead of "Gee, that's great, aren't you wonderful!" I told her I was willing to hear an offer, but this offer was incomplete.

Was this the part of lawyering where you ignore what you don't wish to address? Well, that doesn't work for me, so let's get back to reality.

She rolled her eyes and was inpatient with me, which I couldn't believe. Although I was flipping out on the inside, I saw that I needed to calm my attorney down to make some progress. Are you kidding? Where was the cool professional demeanor that lawyers are supposed to bring to the table? Wasn't this a negotiation, which consists of some back and forth on the issues until an agreement is reached? Did her emotions get the better of her on that day or was she just bad at negotiating? This was the absolute worst time in the two-year-long case for this to come out.

Okay, I'm not seeing great negotiation skills here. I'm seeing mid-level negotiation skills at best. I was also bothered because I didn't see any paperwork in front of her. Maybe the paperwork was in the negotiation room, but she had nothing at all to refer to. Didn't she need a piece of paper, a post-it note, a napkin, or something to scribble on? Was she negotiating the details off the top of her head with nothing to reference? It seemed so. Okay, it's not hard to remember 4 or 5 details, but the case was not limited to 4 or 5 issues. I would expect that no case involves just 4 or 5 issues. Didn't she anticipate having to negotiate the other 8 issues which we discussed for months on end? If they refused those issues shouldn't their refusals be communicated as part of their offer? What were all our emails about? It's been over a YEAR, for goodness sakes. Why are we here if not to resolve *all* the issues which needed to be included in the Separation Agreement? Unbelievable. Perhaps she did a terrific job negotiating those 4-5 issues. I don't know. But in my mind…she was unprepared. Plain and simple.

But I was not. To get through this, I was going to have to push her and insist on some structure. I gave her a copy of my grid to use as a reference. I asked her to go back into the negotiation room and get a response for the remaining issues. I repeated that I would entertain a complete offer. At least now she had something to work from to provide me with a comprehensive offer.

Our negotiation meeting was scheduled for late afternoon. I noticed that both attorneys started to get fidgety as it got closer to 5:00 pm because they wanted to go home. Keep that in mind when you schedule negotiations. Do you have enough time to cover everything? Do you need all-day or perhaps 2 to 3 hours at one sitting is enough? My experience is that it doesn't get completely resolved in a day so breaking up discussions into separate sessions may help. Separate sessions also allow you to consider the offer overnight without having to answer in the moment.

As the day ended, more of the remaining issues were answered. Perhaps not every single issue, but more than were included in the first offer. We stopped around 5:30 pm. That was ok, I was mentally exhausted from the day. The attorneys agreed that opposing counsel would write up a draft of the Separation Agreement.

In my case, I felt my attorney didn't do great negotiating on my behalf. I wasn't in the negotiation room, but the results didn't show an awful lot at first. I had to provide her with structure for what an offer to me should include. I had to push my attorney, which is entirely too damn bad if she didn't like it. I spent a boatload of money to get to this point of negotiation. I deserved better representation and so do you. Remember you are looking out for yourself, not the comfort or convenience of your attorney, or opposing counsel, or your estranged spouse. You are the one who will live with the results from these negotiations.

Offer Grid

I used an offer grid at the negotiation table. It was handwritten, quickly drawn while I was in the adjoining office, and nothing fancy, but it helped me to focus on the details of the offer. I have included a sample offer grid for your use when negotiating. It is broken into sections which include property division, assets, debts, health insurance and so on. Copy the page, or feel free to tailor it as needed to fit your specific case, and then use it.

Everyone is nervous and emotions can run high during negotiations. Having a complete overview of offers keeps things focused and identifies any gaps, hopefully lowering confusion and reducing the possibility of forgetting to include a topic.

I recommend you use the issues on your grid as talking points with your attorney in advance of negotiations to make sure you are both on the same page. You can indicate which points of negotiation are of most important to you.

For his part, I think he ran out of money and had to accept his attorney's recommendation to negotiate.

Sample Offer Grid

	Offer #1	Counteroffer	Offer #2	Counteroffer
	Date/ time:	Date/ time:	Date/ time:	Date/ time:
Children:				
Child custody				
Child support				
Childcare				
Property Distribution				
House				
Furniture				
Electronics				
Car				
Pets				
Assets				
Bank accounts				
Credit Union				
Pension				
Retirement accounts				
Other financial assets				
PayPal/Venmo				
Debts				
Charge cards				
Mortgage				
Car				
Loans				

Financial Arrangements:				
House buyout				
House payments				
Rental lease				
Health insurance				
Life insurance				
Car payments				

My Separation Agreement

After the first negotiation meeting in March, we continued to hammer out details of the Separation Agreement through email until we finally reached an agreement. I made sure to include a stipulation requiring the POS move out of my house within 5 days of signing. About time! He had taken advantage of me long enough and needed to be out.

A separation agreement is required to be notarized, which your attorney usually handles. You will initial each page as well as sign your full name at several places throughout.

My Separation Agreement is 37 pages long and outlines the payments he would receive, including:

- One-time payment of $15,000 to forfeit any claim on my house, due upon signing.
- Yearly payments of $10,000 for 5 years to forfeit his claim to my pension.
- A QDRO for 10% of my retirement account.

The QDRO could have been much higher. Having proof of my separate property claim greatly reduced that amount. As part of QDRO calculations I also received credit for half his annuity which he withdrew as part of his pre-divorce financial manipulations (the clean hands reference).

With one exception, everything else in the Separation Agreement was related to paying him off. Completely unfair, but we've already established that fair is not part of the divorce equation. Paying him meant getting my freedom from his toxic personality and putting an end to this awful situation.

The only concession I received from him was to remain 50% beneficiary on his life insurance policy, contingent upon my paying half the premiums. It was his only asset and I wanted it included in the Separation Agreement. Life insurance is typically not part of divorce negotiations in New York State. My attorney did not want to include it in negotiations and flat out refused to talk about it every time I brought it up. I continued to push, and she continued to argue against it, but it was something I wanted and would not be put aside. I pushed her and insisted. It was added to negotiations and shockingly, opposing counsel did not make a big deal of it.

The Best Strategy

The best strategy is to get through negotiations. In addition to talking to your lawyer about divorce strategy, talk to them about negotiation strategy.

Key Take-Aways:

Every discussion with your attorney is money.

Push your attorney for negotiation.

Write down your negotiation issues for yourself and your attorney.

Discuss what your expected outcomes are.

Write each offer on your negotiation grid to see details clearly.

Negotiation is not a bad word.

- It will save you time.

- It will save you attorney fees.

- It will save you trauma.

Your lawyer still gets paid even if they are unprepared.

Don't be afraid to disagree.

Speak up if you wish for more negotiation on a specific topic.

Take a break if you need it.

Not everything is resolved in one meeting.

More details may come up after initial negotiations.

Remember the adage: Actions speak louder than words.

Remember my personal adage: If it sounds like crap, then it's crap.

Chapter 12:
My Divorce Timeline

Here's a bird's-eye-view of my divorce timeline:

Year 1:

January:	The POS withdrew funds from his annuity account.
	He removed me as beneficiary from his life insurance policy.
	He withdrew my access to his business account.
	These three pre-divorce maneuverings contributed to the court's reference as him not having "clean hands."
	I came home from work one day to an attorney's letter notifying me of the divorce.
February:	I retained an attorney, and we reviewed our case.
	Offer to opposing counsel to negotiate was rejected.
	I filed for divorce.
	Court appearances began and continued every 6 weeks.
March:	Discovery process began.
May:	Discovery pending.

June: Filed subpoenas.

Received notification of the emergency motion filed with the court, requiring an immediate court appearance.

Agreed to a stipulation to pay COBRA in emergency court appearance.

Sent letter to opposing counsel requesting a response to our discovery request.

Started a new job.

July: My response to the emergency motion was filed with the court.

August:We sent another letter to opposing counsel requesting a response to discovery.

September:We sent another letter to opposing counsel requesting a response to discovery.

Received the court's written response to the emergency motion.

October: We submitted additional request for discovery.

We were notified of new opposing counsel.

First court appearance with new opposing counsel. Additional request for discovery.

November: Request for discovery documentation to support business expenses.

December: Received professional appraisal of my house.

Year 2:

January:	Preparing for negotiations.
	Scheduled a sit-down negotiation meeting.
February	Sit-down negotiation meeting held.
March:	Reviewed draft of Separation Agreement.
April:	Revisions to Separation Agreement continued.
May:	Separation Agreement signed and submitted to court.
	POS finally moved out of my house. Halleluiah.
June through September:	Continue paying the attorney each and every month.
October:	Requested my attorney follow up with the court regarding the Judgement of Divorce.
November:	Repeated my request to my attorney to follow up on the Judgement of Divorce.
December:	Received the Judgement of Divorce.
	Finished paying my attorney's bill.
	COBRA payments stopped.
	Merry Christmas.

Ugly, Isn't It?

Please learn from my horror story and don't let it happen to you. Forewarned is forearmed.

Chapter 13:
Surviving Your Emotions

Let's talk about emotions, or more specifically, letting off some pressure and keeping your sanity. Sounds melodramatic, right? But it isn't. It one hundred percent applies with a divorce, or should I say it especially applies to a contested divorce.

Mental health is a big part of divorce. A calm mind is better able to handle it when turmoil is thrown at it. I found it quite stressful to stay on top of changes in the case, provide answers as needed, fulfill latest attorney/court requests, and maneuver through my attorney and the legal process. I was completely overwhelmed, primarily with the divorce, but I also started a new job at that time. Of course, my divorce stress leaked over into my new job.

My divorce brought me to a very dark place. I experienced the full spectrum of emotions, ending every day in physical exhaustion due to emotional exhaustion. I was tired all the time, dragging myself out of bed each day.

If you are at this point, give yourself credit for getting through the day.

Depression

I understand depression better now. How the weight of it bearing down on you feels physical.

In my case, depression was living through an ugly divorce dragging on forever without an end in sight. Seventeen months is a long time. Each day was more miserable than the last while continuing to contend with dirty tricks and money worries. All the while knowing that the next day will be just as miserable, or worse, and trying to brace myself for it. It was impossible to not feel the weight of depression.

The depression during my divorce was the first time in my life I experienced serious depression. I have the utmost empathy for anyone suffering from depression. The accompanying feelings that your life is spiraling out of control and hopelessness add more weight on top of your depression, and you don't know how to get out from under those feelings.

The Fog

My brain is always going and doesn't stop. Is yours? For your sake I hope not because it can be exhausting, especially in a divorce. My decisions sit on my brain, to be reviewed again and again in an endless loop where sometimes you can't break the cycle. The overwhelming trauma of divorce often turned into brain fog where I couldn't concentrate.

The fog is like walking in a pool. It's an effort to move and it takes twice the work to get a few steps forward.

For me the fog was caused by the kaleidoscope of big emotions moving and shifting on a minute-by-minute basis. They sat on top of one another in a big unsustainable pile of overloaded brain circuits. Someone asks you a question at work while your mind is a hundred miles away and you fake a response because you're in a fog.

Panic

Panic is scary, and a panic attack is extremely scary. A panic attack comes on suddenly, you can't control it, and it doesn't instantly go away just because you want it to. While my divorce continued, my anxiety followed pace and increased day by day. For a year my stomach hurt all the time, like a huge knot. I lived the expression "tied into a knot". It was like constantly living with a fight-or-flight adrenaline reaction or the constant feeling of impending doom.

After a year, the panic and anxiety increased to the point that I couldn't bring myself to read my emails at all. I dreaded it. My heart raced and my stomach would drop at the thought. I couldn't handle any more emails or deal with the next ridiculous issue. Usually open, I now kept my email application closed, but that didn't mean the divorce didn't exist. There was always some issue to respond to. Of necessity I began a new routine to read my email only once a day and sometimes it would take the entire day until I was ready to tackle it.

It felt like not even one day went by without having to handle divorce issues. Emails kept coming with more questions, more issues, more inaccurate statements, and more lies to defend against. Email after email from the lawyer — all negative. Emails regarding strategy, documents, or legal strategy, all requiring a response.

My anxiety built anticipating another email, then usually built even larger after reading it, and then figuring out what my response was. Did I make the right choice? Will it help my case? What could happen now? How much would this cost? The mental chaos of dealing with all the details and decisions was substantial. Adding to this were the living conditions at home.

You know you need help, but it can be too overwhelming to even think about. My panic attack before reading the court's response to the emergency motion scared me. It hit home and I realized I couldn't tolerate much more. I reached a point where I knew I had to do something to help myself. Floating along on this wave of big negative emotions was not sustainable.

Self Care

About five months into the divorce process, I started a new job and of course wanted to present my best career self at work.

Sometimes I was successful at presenting my career self and sometimes I was not. The magnitude of the black cloud over your head is hard to turn off like a switch. If I had just read an email from my attorney or followed up on an issue, it was very difficult to make the mental switch back to being an energetic happy new employee eager to learn, be a team player, and produce at the top of my game. My attention was divided and sometimes I was more in my own head than focused on the job. Being an energetic and happy new employee was a stretch. Drained of energy, I admit I wasn't as sharp as I usually pride myself on.

Throughout the divorce proceedings and up until signing the Separation Agreement, the POS lived in my house. He moved into the basement and did not leave. Since he worked from home, I was legally unable to kick him out of my house because if I did, he could sue me for loss of income. Which I knew he would do. He took full advantage of the situation and lived in my basement for 17 months. Except for the internet bill needed for his business, he had stopped paying for any of his living expenses. I was forced to see him walking around my house as if he owned it, free of charge, all while he was thinking of more ways to take advantage of me or to take me down. My living was confined to my bedroom as my only private spot. I was living with the enemy in a war zone. Between home and work I was in a constant state of stress.

It felt like I was falling off a cliff. Literally falling like you see in the movies, with my arms flailing about and nothing to hold on to, and the ground coming up quickly. The trauma was relentless, and I was trying to survive the fall. For a long time, I didn't have energy to do anything at all. But that doesn't work either because you just go further into the black hole where the weight becomes heavier to bear. You reach a critical point and try something to help yourself out of self-preservation, which is what happened to me. Out of necessity I tried to help myself. Not a lot at once, but slowly over time, and anything I did was purely intuitive to minimize that out-of-control falling feeling.

Did it help? Yes, a little bit. Enough that I tried it again. One positive move that built onto a previous positive move to help with the panic and anxiety. It was self-care, but not because I had energy to spare or was interested in self-improvement. Whatever I did allowed my mind to rest for a few precious minutes and helped me survive the day without exploding into a million pieces.

Try some self-care. Although at first it may not feel like it, it will help you work through the darkness to the other side.

Self Care That Helped Me:

Here are some self-care methods which helped me:

Therapy.

- One of the best things I did for myself was to go to therapy. It was hard and painful but helped a tremendous amount. More on that experience later.

Medication.

- I took doctor-prescribed valium to reduce my stress level, although sparingly because while it helped, I was often tired from it which made working difficult.
- I had terrible pains in my stomach for over a year. About nine months in I discovered over-the-counter antacid pills helped to alleviate the constant pain and calm the gigantic lump of agitation in my stomach. Why didn't I think of them sooner?

Music.

- It was a welcome distraction to sooth my mind and put some distance to the details of the divorce.

Walking.

- I took a break during the day to walk for 15-20 minutes. Walking helps to relieve some of the adrenaline and stress in your body. The brain fog temporarily lifts, and some clearer thoughts emerge.

Breathing.

- Deep calming breaths. Four counts in, hold, then eight counts out. I found that structured breathing exercises had a soothing effect.

Prayer.

- Through prayer I was able to voice my desperate feelings without judgment. It doesn't mean I was at peace when I prayed, because it was far from a peaceful conversation on my part, but it helped me inch towards a more peaceful feeling. Without a doubt, it was the lowest point in my life, and I asked God for help to take some of the burden from me. I prayed and felt comforted, it's as simple as that.

I began to establish some self-care routines throughout the day. Although initially I had to force myself, I started to look forward to these small breaks. They gave my brain much-needed rest for a few precious minutes and provided comfort by giving me some in control over my life amid all the craziness.

Explore your own options for self-care.

My Therapy Experience

I came home from work one day to an attorney's letter in the mail with the POS standing nearby advising me to get a divorce lawyer. Although we were not getting along lately, stupid me for being shocked since we had never discussed divorce before. Looking back over our relationship, I should have seen it coming. It was a relatively short conversation that night. He stated that he was divorcing, and that was it. I asked if he would consider marriage counseling and he reluctantly agreed to it. Sounds good, although it turned out to be not so good.

He went to three sessions. He sat with his arms crossed over his chest, wouldn't look at me, and didn't want to answer any of the therapist's questions. So much for participating. He wasn't interested in any discussion, self-reflection, or recognizing any of his feelings of anger or responsibility in any way. To the contrary, he told the therapist to "fix" me because I was 100% at fault.

Wow. This wasn't going well.

During the third session, after the therapist asked him some questions and he gave curt responses, the therapist commented that he looked angry. He didn't like that, said he wasn't mad, then yelled that he wasn't mad. The therapist again tried to talk to him but instead of answering he stood up, said "This is crap," and started to walk out. He looked at me and expected me to walk out with him, but I told him I was staying, which surprised him. He walked out and that was the end of our marriage counseling sessions, and subsequently any further discussion. He had flipped a switch in his brain regarding the marriage and wanted no part of it. There was no coming back. Coincidentally, that was the last time we spoke, although he continued to live in my house for an additional 16 months.

It may have been the end of therapy for him, but it wasn't the end for me. I continued privately with that same therapist for six months.

Overall, it was a positive experience for me and I'm glad I continued. My therapist helped me to work through some of the rawness, and I learned through the experience what therapy is and what therapy is not.

What Therapy Is Not

I had never been to therapy before and didn't know what to expect. The first two months I cried at every session. Unrealistically I thought therapy would magically take away the pain, but that's not what happens.

Therapy is not like ordering off a menu, such as: 20 sessions to happiness, or 10 sessions to overcome your divorce. How nice that would be, but unfortunately, it doesn't work that way. Therapy is not being told you're right or wrong. A therapist doesn't have magic words to take away your troubles, and you don't come out of each therapy session singing a song.

What Therapy Is

Therapy can be painful. Your go to therapy because you're hurting. What a therapist does is validate your pain and guide you to move through it. Therapy is a safe place to talk, and to put a name to the feelings you are having.

You can't remain standing in your pain. The emotions need to come out, or else they eat you alive. A therapist will help you to process the raw feelings and gain some equilibrium. To acknowledge where you are right now in your life and guide you in taking a step forward, which is one step away from the pain. To validate your pain and guide you to move through it.

My therapist brought a different perspective to our sessions. His regular questions included how I was functioning through the day, if I was working, and how I was handling the legal details. One thing he recommended was to have a small script prepared if someone asked of the divorce, which would eliminate surprise and help me to manage the conversation. His perspective helped me through the initial shock and pain, to see there was another side.

Don't expect to take one big leap through all your emotions at once. The therapist walks with you along your journey. You need to put the effort in and work the program. I stated earlier that therapy can be painful, but it's a pain which leads to healing.

I whole-heartedly recommend therapy. It's a helpful pressure relief tool for divorce trauma and it's worth the effort. Don't be hesitant to go to a therapist.

Non-Traditional Therapy

In addition to traditional therapy sessions, I had many non-traditional therapy sessions with my family and friends who listened to me rant and rave, cry and scream, and everything in between. These non-traditional sessions were more frequent than my traditional therapy sessions, and of great value. My family and friends were a terrific support system for me. I'm thankful for each time they reached out and the forbearance shown. It couldn't have been fun for them.

Especially my mother, who heard all the good, the bad, and the ugly, and provided valuable insight and wisdom along the way. Thanks Mom.

I tried to keep it together as much as possible in front of my daughter, but I don't know how successful I was. She saw me fall apart more times than I care to admit, and it wasn't pretty. Thank you, Honey.

Emails of Encouragement

As I was going through my own mess, I stumbled across a website that sends daily inspirational emails each day for the first year of your divorce. At Divorcecare.org, you can sign up for emails which give encouragement and are geared toward what you are experiencing on a day-to-day basis throughout that difficult first year. I found the emails helpful.

Grain of Sand Approach

I realize the advice of taking a walk may sound silly and too insignificant to make a difference while you are drowning in the middle of your divorce trauma and your head is spinning. One action of self-care by itself is not enough to turn things around for you or take away all your stress and anxiety like a magic wand.

Consider what I call the Grain of Sand Approach to survival. Each time you help yourself, one more grain of sand is moved from the negative side over to the positive side. All those positive grains of sand add up and help you to recover and calm your soul.

Key Take-Aways:

Negative emotions weigh you down.

It's an effort to move, like walking in a pool.

It can be overwhelming but taking a step forward will help.

Consider therapy.

Don't overthink it, just do a bit of self-care.

It gives you some control over the current madness.

Start with a walk.

Breathe deeply.

The forced feeling will go away.

Keep at it.

Ask for help if you need it.

Chapter 14:
Costs

Let's examine the costs for your divorce, both tangible and intangible. The cost to your wallet is more obvious, but there is also the cost to your mental health and recovery. How much of each is dependent upon the complexity of your own journey.

Total Cost of Divorce

Your attorney fees depend on the volume and length of your case. The more back and forth emails between you and your attorney, or between your attorney and opposing counsel, the higher the cost. The more documentation, court appearances, subpoenas, and emergency motions, the higher the cost.

Let's review some cold-hard facts on the cost of a divorce, or should I say cold-hard cash.

The Cold-Hard Facts

- Estimate $500 minimum up to $1000 per hour for every email, discussion, and any work from your attorney, including your attorney's review of your case, any communications with opposing counsel, responses to court, etc.

- Estimate $500 or more per hour for review of any financial documentation, whether yours or your spouses.

- Estimate $2,000 for each court appearance, plus attorney parking fees.

- Estimate $500 minimum for each subpoena issued.

- Estimate $15,000 for attorney fees for each motion before the court which includes a court appearance, discussing strategy, researching supporting arguments, drafting, and filing the response.

- Estimate $25,000 for an initial trial retainer. Keep in mind this is only a starting point and be assured you will need to replenish in large amounts throughout the trial.

Estimated Costs by Divorce Strategy

Recall the different strategies outlined for obtaining a divorce. Let's apply the previous rough estimates to each option for a real understanding of cost:

1. With option 1, mediation, I would guesstimate $5,000-$10,000 is possible for an uncontested Separation Agreement, dependent upon the level of complexity. It could be even less if you and your spouse file the court paperwork yourselves, which is an option.

2. With option 2, negotiation, I would guesstimate $10,000 to $35,000 for a Separation Agreement if both parties can successfully negotiate.

3. With option 3, going-for-the-jugular, I would guesstimate $35,000 to $100,000 for a Separation Agreement. How much money you'll spend depends on how much time it takes before you smarten up and start negotiating in earnest. Are you paying $75,000 in attorney fees to win $35,000?

4. With option 4, a trial, I would estimate a minimum of $100,000-$125,000 to go to trial. And that is just to start the trial. A trial is not immediately agreed to by the court. Prepare to pay at least that amount to wind your way along the yellow brick road until the Judge grants a trial. A closer estimate is probably $150,000 or more.

Then there are the costs of an actual trial. It would be at least $25,000 for the initial trial retainer, with the same amount for each installment throughout the trial. The retainer would be spent down at a modest rate of $5,000-$7,000 per day for estimated prep and court time. And that's for one attorney. Multiply that as needed if additional attorneys are assisting with the trial. I would say a trial would be another $100,000 minimum.

Don't forget that with a trial, the court decides the division of assets and neither you nor your spouse have any say in the matter.

Keep in mind these are estimates only, based on $500 per hour attorney fees. If your attorney's hourly rate is higher the estimates increase accordingly.

As an example, let's say you're planning on painting a room and changing the flooring, and have estimated X amount to complete your project. You start but for various reasons additional charges are added to the budget. You find that more work is required, or more time is required, or more resources are required, and you ended up spending more than you originally thought. When was the last time a project came in under budget? Apply that same situation to your divorce. Something will come up and it will cost more than you anticipated.

Food for thought.

So How Much Will You Spend on Your Divorce?

Most divorces do not end in trial. Who could afford it? It takes many months, or more likely years, of steadfast legal maneuvering and refusal to negotiate. I venture that the average divorcing couple does not have such assets to throw away. You need big money for a trial. Trial is a last resort, so let's eliminate that option in a discussion of costs.

My divorce fell into the going-for-the-jugular option, which, knowing my husband's nature, I anticipated from the beginning, although I couldn't possibly anticipate to what extent. I filed the initial summons with the court to protect myself. The court's guidance seemed like a good thing. I anticipated the divorce might be messy and hoped the court's oversight would be helpful to work things out. Even with that hope I thought my divorce would end in a few months, maybe six months tops. As it turned out it took about a year longer than I anticipated. I miscalculated the opposing side's tactic to draw out the process so completely until the money ran out. What a waste.

Although the actual court process moves along slowly, the bills move along very quickly. My attorney's fees were about $4,000 to $7,000 per month, which of course, I couldn't afford. Who could? I wrote the monthly checks against my home equity account until that was maxed out. Then I paid my lawyer in monthly installments for another year until my account was paid. Only a crazy person would want their divorce to last so long and cost so much.

The average person getting a divorce cannot afford the going-for-the-jugular option, and I suspect that includes you. Ask yourself, is it worth it? What is $50,000 or $75,000 worth to you? Is your anger worth $75,000? Is the need to punish your spouse worth $50,000 to you? Wouldn't you rather have that money for yourself? I can tell you that attorneys do not waive even one penny of their fees, and their retainer probably includes a clause that fees not paid by a certain date are subject to interest.

In a divorce the money adds up too quickly. Think about keeping at least part of it instead of using it up in attorney fees. My advice would be to generate less attorney bills, get out of debt faster, and go on a trip to the Caribbean. That's preferable to spending it on a long, drawn-out divorce.

The options available to you to avoid a long, drawn-out divorce are either mediation or negotiation.

If negotiating with your estranged spouse will ultimately save you money, should you try? Even if it means eating some relationship crow, or letting their ego have the 'win'? Or not punishing them for what happened in the past? Is it worth giving some money in negotiation to get to a Separation Agreement? Of course, it is! Who cares if they think they're right if it saves you money in the long run? You are getting divorced, so their sense of right or wrong shouldn't matter to you. They are not going to come around to your way of thinking, and realize they are in the wrong.

Do they think their actions are justified? Yes.

Do they think they are right? Probably.

Are you going to change their mind? Probably not.

You won't be able to prove them wrong, so don't try. Save yourself the trauma. And the money.

At this point, drawing out the divorce won't change anything and you're still getting divorced. Best to accept that reality and move it along. The going-for-the-jugular option will cost you tens of thousands of additional dollars. Your efforts would be better spent acknowledging your situation, working through the big emotions, and focusing on the division of assets.

The "why" of the divorce is best left to visits with your therapist, family, or friends. Write less checks to your attorney and vent to your dog. Your goal is to get through negotiations. Think about speaking directly to your spouse to arrive at a settlement. If you can't speak to your spouse, then push your attorney to negotiate an offer with opposing counsel. Push your attorney to negotiation on every single phone call.

My apologies if I am going on and on regarding the financial cost of a messy divorce. I would rather have kept the money spent on attorney fees for my divorce, or even salvaged half of what was wasted.

You will too when all this is over.

Emotional Cost

The emotional cost of a divorce is very real. Do what you can to help yourself.

- Figure out how to accept the situation.
- Figure out how to divide the assets.
- Work on strengthening your case.
- Work toward establishing separate property if applicable.
- Remember self-care.
- Time will help to metabolize that big pile of hard emotions in your gut.

Total Cost

I have put off writing this section because it's too scary and depressing to actual type the words, but I am committed to honestly represent my nightmare, and you need to hear it, so here I go:

The total cost of my divorce was over $100,000, consisting of:

- $20k for COBRA payments, and
- $80k in attorney fees.

That $100,000 total brought me through my Separation Agreement to the Judgement of Divorce, which does not include the payments specified in the agreement.

I'm angry and sad that my divorce got to such a point and cost a ridiculously extreme amount of money. I have lost countless nights of sleep over it as I continue to work through the after-effects.

Lingering Effects

Effects from a divorce, especially a contested divorce, hang around long after receiving your Judgement of Divorce. Having been through divorce twice, I see the vast differences between an uncontested and a contested divorce. The contested divorce has exponentially more lingering effects than an uncontested one.

For my contested divorce, the lingering effects are both financial and emotional.

Financially, I will be paying for my divorce for years to come, in addition to also paying the POS a yearly amount. I estimate it will take me 10 years to pay off my divorce. If I had known at the onset of my divorce what it would cost, I would have presented the POS with a 'take this and go away' offer. It would have been much preferable to what happened. Knowing him, he wouldn't have taken the offer since he was so focused on getting a pot of gold.

Emotionally, I am changed. My tolerance for negativity is limited. My ability to process negativity is now limited. It's like I overdosed on stress and trauma for too long and can now only take it in small doses. The physical reaction to stress which I experienced during the divorce comes roaring back at times, and I must step away and distance myself from it. Turn the channel, stop reading the news article, or change the subject. I'm sure I have PTSD, which started around 6 months into the divorce process. It has gotten a bit better over time, but I can't say if it will ever go away completely. I doubt it.

I stumbled upon a trick which helped redirect my thoughts during the times my brain couldn't stop thinking negative divorce thoughts. To distract myself I picked a song to sing in my head. The first song that popped into my mind was "Take Me Out to the Ballgame." Short and sweet, it worked to divert my thoughts and allowed me to focus on something else. Give it a try, and sing it as often as needed.

Key Take-Aways:

When emotions are high, money is high.

How much is the attorney's bill now?

I can't afford this.

How to stop the madness?

Trying to negotiate doesn't cost, it saves.

Swallow your pride if that will save you money.

Let's get this done.

Chapter 15:
The Right and Wrong of It

Looking back, could things have been handled differently by both of us? Yes, both in the marriage but most especially, in the divorce. Unfortunately, his greed was ultimate and his refusal to negotiate cost a whole lot of money, but I should have tried any way I could to change the trajectory.

Never having been through a contested divorce before, of course I didn't know what to expect. Isn't that why you have a lawyer? In my case, mistakes were made by all, for which I am paying dearly. I am living with and take responsibility for my decisions along the way, but unfortunately, the POS's personality does not allow him to take accountability for his.

After great reflection, here are the mistakes made by each during my divorce. These are my lessons learned throughout my ordeal. Hopefully they can provide you with some awareness as you travel down your own yellow brick road to divorce.

What He Did Wrong

(I'll limit my responses to the divorce only).

- Pre-divorce financial maneuvers.

- Never discussing divorce with me before starting the process with an attorney.

- Advised me we were getting a divorce through an attorney's letter.

- Walked out on marriage counselling.

- Took advantage and lived in my basement free of charge during the divorce proceedings.

- Stopped payment for any of his living expenses.

- Complete disregard for financial help I've given him in the past.

- Used divorce proceedings as punishment.

- His greed.

- Encouraging and fostering harassment from his attorney.

- Made false statements to the court.

- Fabricated his expenses.

- Lying in his *Statement of Net Worth*.

- Not accepting excellent health insurance of my new job.

- Forcing me to pay COBRA payments for his insurance.

- Submitted an unnecessary motion to the court.

- His arrogance in making demands of the Judge (although it ultimately benefited me).

- Not including an explanation for removing annuity money in his final response to the emergency motion.

- Lied any way that would benefit him.

- Careful planning to take advantage of me.

- Used underhanded tactics every chance he could.

- Believed his own lies.

- Wasted a whole lot of my money due to inability to negotiate.

What My Attorney Did Wrong

- Did not advise me she was changing law firms.

- Claimed great negotiation skills.

- Suggested COBRA payments ending at Judgement of Divorce instead of a calendar end date.

- Lack of strategic thinking to issue subpoenas to document POS's pre-divorce financial maneuvering.

- Not issuing subpoenas to bank for missing account statements.

- Was waiting for trial to issue subpoenas for missing discovery documentation.

- Extended the divorce process by allowing 4-6 weeks between each discovery request.

- Arguing with me regarding submitting a Motion for Discovery.

- Complacently went along with the long-term divorce strategy.

- Not once commiserated that the divorce was going on too long or cost too much.

- Not once giving explanation why it was taking so long.

- Not strategizing how to shorten the divorce process.

- Allowing opposing counsel to harass me.

- Fought me to include his life insurance asset as part of negotiations.

- Ignored all requests to get him out of my house.

- Not enough pushback, if any, to opposing counsel.

- Not prepared with a list of issues for negotiations.

- Unimpressive negotiation skills.

- Expected my immediate compliance with opposing counsel's negotiation offer.
- Not following up on length of time it was taking to get the Judgement of Divorce issued by the court.
- Complacently travelling along the yellow brick road to divorce.
- Not pushing for negotiation.
- Not pushing for negotiation.
- Not pushing for negotiation.

What I Did Wrong

- Not getting a pre-nup.
- Not listening to my inner voice.
- Believing he had character.
- Believing he would keep the vow he made 'on his honor'.
- During the marriage, paid bills for separate property out of a marital bank account.
- Filing joint tax returns during the marriage.
- Was stupidly shocked by divorce.
- Not recognizing how ruthless he could be.
- Believed he would end the marriage fairly.
- Believed he would end the marriage without lies.
- Believing my attorney when she said she was a good negotiator.
- Not pushing my attorney hard enough for negotiation.
- Not trying to speak directly to my spouse to negotiate.
- Agreed to COBRA payments with open end date, instead of a calendar end date.
- Not bringing all my attorney's mistakes to her attention.
- Not taking charge to resolve my attorney's mistakes.
- Not forcing the issue to file a Motion of Discovery.
- Not changing my attorney.
- Not changing my attorney.
- Not changing my attorney.

What I Did Right

- Although he repeatedly asked, I never put his name on the deed to my house. Thank God.

- Got up every day and went to work in the middle of divorce trauma.

- Not treating my lawyer as a therapist.

- Was active in my own defense.

- Keeping my own paperwork.

- Pushed my attorney to issue subpoenas early in the process. (That saved the day.)

- Was able to prove his false statements to the court.

- Forced some issues with my attorney.

- Would not back down from including life insurance in negotiations.

- Created negotiation grid to stay focused and reduce emotions during negotiations.

- Would not accept a partial offer.

- Required attorney to present a complete offer.

- Created retirement timeline to support separate property claim.

- Started some self-care.

- Saved money by representing myself for the QDRO.

- Recognized the blessing of not living with a street fighter anymore.

- Reclaimed my house when he finally moved out.

Chapter 16:
Moving On

Has your spouse moved out, or have you moved out? If so, good. It needs to be that way when you're getting a divorce. The alternative is much worse.

The POS lived in my basement for the entire 17 months until the Separation Agreement was signed, with one year of that time free of charge. Since his office was in the house, I had no legal recourse to get him to leave my house. He was only too happy to take advantage of the situation and felt no hesitation to mooch off me for that entire time.

His presence filled up the whole house; the air was heavy and oppressive. Instead of a safe place, my home was uncomfortable to live in and was now a battle ground. For the entire duration of the divorce proceedings, I lived in my bedroom as much as possible to avoid the common areas. My bedroom was my office as I prepared my defense and organized discovery documentation. It was my dining room where I ate my meals. It was my den for watching tv. I told my family I wasn't afraid to be alone in the house with him, but at times I was. He was getting more and more out of control, and I didn't know what to expect. A few months in, a friend fixed the lock on my bedroom door, and I was able to start locking the door which gave me a tremendous feeling of safety. I locked myself into the sanctuary of my bedroom every night.

While living in my house, the POS's sole purpose was to break me and take me down any way he could. He wouldn't have given a second thought if he had caused me to lose the home I've worked for my entire life. He would have felt it was justified, but for what, I don't know. To say it was stressful does not even touch upon the reality of living like that for 17 months. It took 17 months to end a 17-year marriage. Perhaps there is some weird cosmic symmetry with that. Or maybe the POS was just unhinged.

Back to you. Either your spouse has moved out, or you have, and it feels weird, huh? I understand. The place seems empty and lonely, even factoring in the bad situation it was beforehand. Let's acknowledge how different it is and the weirdness of it.

You're in limbo, which although not ideal, is necessary right now. This is the time to resolve your situation, achieve the goal, and then start recovery. Consider it a breathing space in your life. Maybe recognizing the need for this pause will alleviate the feeling of weirdness.

Personally, I am enjoying the absence of hostility in my house. Hostility has a feeling to it, which I am only too happy to see the end of. For the first time in a long time, I can take a deep breath in my house. I can move around freely and am taking back my space.

Allow yourself some time to recover from this change and to reclaim your life.

Reclaiming your life sounds great, but how exactly do you do that? The answer is…gradually. Gradually you retrain your thoughts. Gradually your mind calms somewhat and you start having more thoughts of the future than thoughts of the past. Gradually your life becomes your own again.

Time Heals

The past can haunt you, but at some point, you need to make the decision to stop allowing the past to dominate your thoughts and to start thinking about the future. It is a conscious decision which will take repeated reminders to yourself. Redirect your mind, even if only for a short time.

Don't be worried if your step forward ends up being a step back. It's part of the process. You take forward and backward steps until the forward steps outweigh the backward steps, and you gain momentum.

Key Take-Aways:

Your spouse leaves, or you leave.

It feels weird, but it's for the best.

Give yourself time to acclimate.

Finish the divorce then take back your life.

Stay with it.

Chapter 17:
Recommendations

Better or Worse

- Is a divorce negotiated in two years better or worse than one that takes two months?
- Is the impact to your life better or worse with a divorce that takes years?
- Is the emotional trauma better or worse with a divorce that takes years?
- Is the cost better or worse with a divorce that takes years?

My answer to all the above questions is…worse.

Key Take-Aways:

You will not get a 100% win.

Justice will not be served.

The court will not punish your spouse for being an idiot.

Meanness is not a factor of divorce.

Punishing your spouse through divorce is the same as flushing money down the toilet.

The rightness or wrongness of their actions mean nothing.

The court sees it as black and white, to be divided.

Do what you can to stop the madness.

Finish it, preferably sooner rather than later.

Push your attorney to negotiate.

The best you can hope for is a partial win.

You don't have to instantly agree to all negotiation offers.

It's ok to take time to consider an offer.

When you're going through hell, keep going.

The limbo phase is necessary to get to the other side.

Then rebuild your life.

Time helps.

The only way out is through.

Chapter 18:
At the End of the Day

Taking Care of Business

After all is said and done, and after the Judgement of Divorce, finish off this legal phase of your life by making additional changes as applicable:

- Change your will to remove the ex-spouse (this is important!).
- Change the beneficiary on any life insurance policies.
- Remove spouse from your health insurance policy.
- Remove spouse from your bank accounts, credit cards, and any other financial accounts.

Final Thoughts

It took me 17 months to get to a Separation Agreement, followed by 7 months to get a Judgement of Divorce, and then 15 months to write about it. My hope is that my experience, disastrous as it was, helps you to navigate the yellow brick road to your own divorce.

Everyone gets to Emerald City in the end. This is about making the journey a little easier.

Good luck.